BLACK is the New GREEN

ALSO BY ARTHUR BLACK

Basic Black (1981)
Back to Black (1987)
That Old Black Magic (1989)
Arthur! Arthur! (1991)
Black by Popular Demand (1993)
Black in the Saddle Again (1996)
Black Tie and Tales (1999)
Flash Black (2002)
Black & White and Read All Over (2004)
Pitch Black (2005)
Black Gold (2006)
Black to the Grindstone (2007)
Planet Salt Spring (audio CD, 2009)

BLACK is the New GREEN

ARTHUR BLACK

HARBOUR PUBLISHING

Harbour Publishing Co. Ltd.
P.O. Box 219, Madeira Park, BC, V0N 2H0
www.harbourpublishing.com

Edited by Susan Mayse
Cover photograph by Howard Fry
Cover design by Anna Comfort
Printed and bound in Canada on 100% PCW recycled paper using soy-based ink

Harbour Publishing acknowledges financial support from the Government of Canada through the Book Publishing Industry Development Program and the Canada Council for the Arts, and from the Province of British Columbia through the BC Arts Council and the Book Publishing Tax Credit.

THE CANADA COUNCIL | LE CONSEIL DES ARTS
FOR THE ARTS | DU CANADA
SINCE 1957 | DEPUIS 1957

BRITISH COLUMBIA
ARTS COUNCIL
Supported by the Province of British Columbia

Library and Archives Canada Cataloguing in Publication

Black, Arthur
   Black is the new green / by Arthur Black.

ISBN 978-1-55017-494-6

   1. Canadian wit and humor (English). I. Title.

PS8553.L318B522 2009   C818'.5402   C2009-903474-3

CONTENTS

YOUR ROVING ROBOREPORTER

ARTHUR IN LIMBOLAND

A STARFISH AT A TIME

HEADING FOR THE
BRIGHT LIGHTS

You probably didn't notice it, because the earth didn't move or anything, but there was a moment a few years ago when everything on our planet changed, probably forever.

Sometime one April—or maybe it was June, or November, we'll never know for sure—but sometime, a farm kid from Maple Creek moved into an apartment in Regina; or perhaps it was a Mexican "illegal" bedding down under a bridge in El Paso; or maybe an Irish Sweepstakes winner from Kilkenny took possession of a mansion in upscale Dublin—somebody, somewhere, moved from the country to a city and tipped the scales.

When that person moved in, it became official. Humankind became more urban than rural. A greater percentage of us now live under the bright lights than out in the boonies.

And that has never happened before.

It's not necessarily a bad thing, given our tendency to foul our own nests. If we're going to make a mess, it's probably better to keep it concentrated in a few spots rather than polluting and desecrating the entire landscape.

But it will change our natures forever. And it will change our cities too.

For one thing, most of those moves weren't made to the downtown core. People are actually moving to the outskirts of cities, where land and housing are still (relatively) cheap and available. City centres are already crowded. They've got nowhere to expand but up, and that option has obvious limitations.

So the outskirts are bulging. The so-called Riots of Paris a few years back didn't take place in any Paris you'd find in a tourist brochure or Michelin Guide. They weren't burning cars and smashing windows along the Champs Elysée. The unrest exploded in the slummy and hideous outskirts of Paris where 75 percent of Parisians live.

After passing the Bienvenidos to Mexico City signs, you can drive for more than an hour through overcrowded Third World barrios before you reach anything resembling the city's core.

Most of the citizens in Istanbul, Turkey, and São Paulo, Brazil, do not live even close to their city centres. Their homes are kilometres away in the swarming, sprawling outskirts.

It's the same the world over. Fifty percent of Barcelonans live in the outskirts, as do almost half the people of Warsaw.

Meanwhile, what's happening to our downtowns? Well, they're changing too. The ones that haven't already been "modernized" are trying to capitalize on their tourist cachet, which is to say their quaintness and historical significance.

They are, in fact, turning into museums of their former selves.

It is still possible to live downtown, but it's pricey and getting pricier. Ask a New Yorker. Or a Venetian. It's hard to think of cities as an endangered species, but if there is such a classification, Venice is surely its poster child.

Basically Venice shouldn't even be there. It's built on 118

tiny islands situated on a marshy lagoon with the Adriatic Sea lapping at its doorstep. Venice has been sinking—or rather flooding—for at least a century. Experts now think they've finally got a handle on the problem and the city has been pronounced safe.

Pending global warming, of course.

Now that they've figured out how to keep the burg afloat, Venetian city fathers face a brand new problem.

The people are leaving.

In the past fifty years the population of the city has shrivelled from 121,000 to just 62,000, a drop of nearly 50 percent. In the past ten years, Venetians have been packing up and moving out at the rate of eight hundred a year. If it keeps up at this pace, the city will be completely devoid of residents by 2046.

Venice council housing chief Mara Rumiz fears her city is approaching the point of no return.

"Beyond then," she says, "Venice will never again be a normal city but will become a mere tourist destination and lose its charm—even for the tourists."

Ah, there's the rub. How much can a city tart itself up and trick itself out before it loses its intrinsic allure and becomes little more than a tacky, barren photo op? Seems to me that's already happened to cities like Reno. And Niagara Falls.

And what do we do after we turn our cities into uninhabitable tourist traps?

Where do we move next?

AROUND THE WORLD ON MUSCLE POWER

So what have you been up to the past couple of years?

If you're like me the answer is, "Same old, same old. Nothing much. Workeatsleep. Couple of car trips, a bout of the flu . . . walked the dogs . . . read some books . . . mowed the grass . . . passed the time."

For Colin Angus and his fiancée Julie Wafeai, the past two years have been somewhat more eventful. They went around the world.

I mean the entire planet. These two thirty-somethings circumnavigated the globe. And what's truly amazing is that they did it without expending an eyedropper's worth of gasoline, diesel or aviation fuel. They circled the planet using only the power of their legs and arms and backs.

There were three of them when they started off from Vancouver in June 2004 on mountain bikes laden like pack mules, heading north. Angus's friend Tim Harvey was on board then too. The original plan was for Angus and Harvey to make the round-the-world trip together. Angus's fiancée Julie was merely going to do the first leg, cycling to Alaska "to keep them company." By early summer Julie was back in Vancouver.

Meanwhile, in Whitehorse, Angus and Harvey trade in their bikes for canoes and paddle fifteen hundred kilometres down the Yukon River to Fairbanks, Alaska. There they switch to an ocean-going rowboat and row another sixteen hundred kilometres to the Alaska coast and the Bering Sea.

Once they get to salt water, rowing the mere eight hundred kilometres across the Bering Sea to Russia is a piece of cake.

Angus and Harvey then spend two months hiking 850 kilometres across the trackless Siberian wastes. Angus has to take the month of December off for surgery, but by January he rejoins Harvey and they cycle, ski and trudge toward Moscow.

Travel under adverse conditions is usually a bonding experience, but not always. Somewhere between northeastern Siberia and the outskirts of Moscow, the two men get to bickering and fall out. They decide they will go their separate ways. It takes Angus six months to make it to Moscow. Harvey, who arrives two months later, will go on to complete the journey on his own.

But for Colin Angus, support is at hand. His fiancée Julie flies to Moscow and rejoins him. Together they bicycle from Moscow to Lisbon, Portugal, in just forty-nine days—a gruelling average of 110 kilometres a day.

Nothing like a change of pace after a 5,500-kilometre ride—Colin and Julie switch to a rowboat, point the prow Columbus-like toward the New World and start rowing. It is late September 2005. Which is to say, hurricane season.

I'll spare you the details. Suffice to say that after four cyclones, uncounted storms and 146 days in a seven-metre rowboat, Colin Angus and Julie Wafeai make it to the Caribbean island of St. Lucia. They rest and take on supplies. Then they're back in the boat and rowing to Costa Rica, a mere twenty-four hundred kilometres farther west. From there, a trifling bike ride of six thousand kilometres fetches them up in Vancouver in front of a totem pole at Kitsilano Point—the very spot they set out from twenty-three months earlier.

Julie Wafeai goes in the record books as the first Canadian woman to do what Columbus did five centuries ago—cross the Atlantic. Except that Julie did it with even more primitive technology than Columbus. Chris had sails and wind power; Julie just had a pair of oars and a strong back.

And Colin Angus becomes the first person in history to circumnavigate the earth using only muscle power.

If these two were Americans, Brits or Aussies, they'd have movie deals, cross-country speaking tours and their own TV series. But this is Canada, eh? The day after they cycled into Vancouver, their incredible story made page four of my morning newspaper, just above the Canadian Tire garden tractor ad. I haven't heard a word about them since.

Why'd they do it? They're greenies. Angus says they wanted "to draw attention to environmentally responsible forms of transportation and the need to reduce greenhouse gas emissions."

Fair enough. We've all heard plenty of politicians and environmental spokesthingies contribute to global warming as they preached that particular sermon.

But these are two folks who walked the walk, not to mention pedalled, paddled and rowed it.

Too bad they're Canadian. They'd be heroes anywhere else.

CONFESSIONS OF AN ECOSINNER

onfession time: You are reading the words of one lousy global citizen. The carbon footprint I leave behind is more like a full-body face plant. I don't drive a hybrid automobile. I burn actual wood in my fireplace that sends actual smoke up my chimney. I leave lamps (bearing taboo incandescent bulbs) burning needlessly in my wake and lazily put my computer on standby while I fix myself a snack from the refrigerator—the door of which, as my better half likes to point out, I leave ajar more often than not.

Bicycle? Yes, I have one. The last time I threw a leg over it was three prime ministers ago. I'm bad. I'm a backslider. An ecosinner. Al Gore would not have me in for green tea.

On the other hand, I'm trying. I've turned over a new leaf. Or a blade, if you like. I bought myself a push lawnmower.

Actually, it's no sacrifice at all—I like my push mower. In an earlier incarnation I owned a house surrounded by half a hectare of lawn. I spent most Saturdays (and often one or two weekday evenings) grumpily prowling across that green expanse on a big, noisy, smelly riding lawnmower that cost me a fortune in gas and threatened to chew my foot off if I ever made a miscue. When I moved to a new house with less lawn, I sold the riding monster and bought a standard gas mower, but I found it was just as smelly and even noisier.

My salvation came at a garage sale a couple of years ago in the form of a Lee Valley push mower. "How much for the mower?" I asked the guy wearing the change apron.

"Twenty bucks, no GST," the man said. I gave him a double sawbuck and I haven't looked back since.

I have been cutting the lawn with my push mower for two years now, and here is what I've learned:

(1) Mowing the lawn need not be undertaken in clouds of noxious exhaust fumes that cry out for a haz-mat suit. A guy pushing a muscle-powered mower actually gets to breathe clean, unpolluted air, not to mention getting first dibs on the delicious scent of new-mown grass.

(2) Mowing the lawn does not have to be a blitzkrieg assault on the eardrums. Instead of that deafening roar of a gas-powered mower, the push mower produces only the delicate flutter and whir of the rotating reel. Instead of **RRRRRRRRRRRRRRRR** you get ffff-frrrrrrrrrrrrrrrrrtttttt. It's a beautiful, comforting sound and it's not loud enough to tick off your neighbours—or even to interrupt the chatter of the robins and finches.

(3) It's way cheaper to operate a push mower. At a time when the cost of a litre of gas is approaching the price of a dollop of Chanel No. 5, the push mower requires exactly zero gas and no oil, aside from a squirt of WD-40 every few months to keep things loosey-goosey.

(4) The lawn looks better after it's been cut with a push mower. The experts say that's because the push mower clips the blades of grass, unlike the power mowers, which slash the grass like a Viking berserker on meth. The end result is a lawn that looks like it's been sculpted by a hair stylist, not clear-cut by an army barber.

(5) You know how many people maim themselves with lawn mowers each year in North America? Over eighty thousand. The injuries range from debris in the eyes through perforated eardrums to full-scale (if amateur) amputations of hands and feet. Wanna guess how many of those injuries come from push mowers? Exactly none. The push mower is the clumsy man's friend.

(6) Although it sounds counterintuitive, it is actually easier to cut the lawn with a push mower. If you're muttering "Hah!" or an even less polite word right now, that's probably because you're remembering those old iron-wheeled, wooden-shafted beasts we both grew up with. Push mowers aren't like that anymore. The modern ones are super-efficient and light as a feather. Some of them weigh as little as three kilograms. Cutting the lawn with a modern push mower isn't an ordeal. More like a stroll in the park.

Now don't think I'm kidding myself. I know that the adoption of push mowers does not spell planetary salvation. The fact that I flutter around my lawn once a week with an unmotorized machine will not put Canada on track to meet its Kyoto requirements.

But it's a start. And it's healthy for me and my lawn. And a darned pleasant way to spend an hour once a week.

IN PRAISE OF THE SIESTA

The late, great Sir Noël Coward wrote many witty and memorable lines, but perhaps his most famous contribution was "Mad dogs and Englishmen go out in the midday sun."

I'm not sure that it marks a great leap forward for humankind, but it looks like forty-four million Spaniards may be about to join those batty Brits and crazed canines. The Spanish government is officially abolishing the siesta.

Siesta. A beautiful word for a beautiful concept. It comes from *hora siesta*, "sixth hour," referring to the number of hours after dawn when it seems like a good idea to get out of the potato patch, turn off the cement mixer, abandon the Toro mower and get your carcass out of the broiling sun and into some nice cool shade. It's just a sensible break, not the end of the working day. The workers return refreshed to their jobs for a couple of hours in the cooler temperatures of the evening.

The Spanish didn't invent the siesta—they swiped it from Portugal—but they enthusiastically exported it to grateful nations around the world. Mexicans embrace the siesta concept, as do most Central and South American countries as well as the Philippines. Indeed any country where the mercury routinely soars into the 40s Celsius in the early afternoon usually observes some variation of the siesta. Most folks in China, Taiwan and southern India also make it a point to pull down the shades just after lunch.

Not that the Spanish siesta is all about sleeping; it's more about family. For untold generations, Spaniards have retired to their homes for a midafternoon break to be with their loved ones, eat a hearty lunch, drink some vino and . . . what have you. The siesta is healthful, life-affirming and pleasant. So naturally the Spanish government wants to get rid of it.

Because it's frightfully unproductive, don't you see? All those citizens enjoying themselves at home when they could be down at the factory cranking out widgets, sweating over hay bales out in the south forty or filling out purchase orders in quintuplicate back at the office.

Let's face it. The siesta is an anachronism. A throwback to ancient times when people lived for themselves, not for the clock on the wall. All that's changed now. Spain is a member of the European Common Market, and how's that going to work if an olive oil importer in Düsseldorf calls Malaga to place an order and all he gets is a busy signal because Senor Malaga has his phone off the hook so it doesn't interrupt his siesta?

Well, no more. Under a new law, federal employees are obliged to take no more than forty-five minutes for lunch and to leave the office for the day no later than 6:00 p.m.

Will it work? I have my doubts. The law was passed one January, when afternoon temperatures are chilly, even downright frigid, in Spain. Spaniards might not think working through the afternoon is a good idea in the torrid summer weather.

As a Luddite and a romantic, I hope the initiative fails miserably. Why should Spain be like Belgium and Denmark and Latvia, all in the name of economic harmonization? German marks and Dutch pfennigs, French francs and Spanish pesetas are already currency history, replaced by the dreary, ubiquitous Euro. Sure, it's easier to figure out what you're paying for a product in Europe now—but it's a whole lot blander.

I guess this is the global village Marshall McLuhan prophesied. No doubt one day Toronto will be just like Toledo and Madrid will be indistinguishable from Moncton.

It's already happening. I spent some time in a town called Almunecar on Spain's Costa del Sol this past winter. Overall the town is unremarkable, except for one section I discovered by accident. It's a labyrinthine warren of twisting cobbled streets that follow no pattern, curving back and even bisecting themselves at times. The streets meander crazily, opening up on unexpected plazas, tiny hidden cafés and ancient churches.

It's the Old Town, originally settled by Phoenicians more than two thousand years ago. It's impossible not to get lost in the Old Town, but it's not very scary because it's not very big. Sooner or later you'll run into something familiar.

Too familiar, actually. After stumbling along one corkscrew alley for a while I suddenly came to an opening.

It was a mini-mall. A nest of shops selling Timex watches, Nike running shoes, Levi's, Jantzen swimwear and Paula Abdul CDs.

On the plus side, I couldn't buy any of it. It was two in the afternoon, and the shops were all closed.

Siesta, don't you know.

AS BUTTERFLiES FLUTTER BY

*They are the bimbos of the natural world: more
beautiful and less interesting, arguably, than other
orders of animals. An evolutionary experiment in
sheer decorative excess, with a high ratio of surface
to innards.*

Those are the words of ecologist David Quamenn, and he's
talking about butterflies. More beautiful for sure—but less
interesting? Mr. Quamenn has impeccable scientific creden-
tials, but I would argue him to the mat on that one. Consider
the annual miracle that unfolds from the Queen Charlottes to
Newfoundland and from the High Arctic to the backyards of
Windsor, Ontario.

This is the migration of the monarchs, the butterflies a lot of
Canucks call King Billy because their colours are those of King
William of Orange. These gobsmackingly beautiful creatures
with their blazing orange and black filigree wings dipsy-doodle
into Canadian meadows and roadsides, backyards and vacant
lots—anywhere, in fact, that milkweed grows. Milkweed and
only milkweed is where monarchs lay their eggs. Milkweed and
only milkweed is what monarch caterpillars eat.

There's an excellent reason for that. Milkweed contains a poison that makes potential predators of monarchs throw up. The gaudy body colours serve as a reminder to birds, frogs, toads and salamanders not to mess with monarchs.

What's more, if the monarch you see is a female, she will be finishing the final leg of a six-thousand-kilometre migration begun by that butterfly's great-grandmother a year earlier. After it lays its eggs, a monarch lives for only about six weeks. Four generations of butterflies may have lived and died on the journey, and yet millions of monarch descendants find their way unerringly to the same grove of trees in a high-mountain forest in Mexico, year after year. A grove they've never seen.

Less interesting, Mr. Quamenn?

It's a perilous journey. The monarchs face hurricanes, tornadoes, freak blizzards, flash floods and droughts, not to mention herbicides, pesticides, and speeding cars, trucks and airplanes. An adverse wind can blow them irretrievably out to sea. A tiny miscalculation flying south can maroon them in Florida or drown them in the Gulf of Mexico. Yet somehow, every year, a critical mass of these creatures manages to find a narrow, eighty-kilometre gap of cool river valleys in Texas that funnels them down to wintering grounds in the Transvolcanic Mountains of Mexico, where they roost semi-dormant in the chilly air that prevails at three thousand metres above sea level.

Somehow—and scientists are baffled by this, because an insect just wouldn't seem to have the requisite mental equipment—monarch butterflies possess the knowledge to orient themselves in latitude and longitude.

It took humans until the eighteenth century to figure out how to do that.

Bimbos, Mr. Quamenn?

It is truly a miracle, but one wonders how much longer the monarchs can pull it off. Farmers loathe the monarch staple—milkweed. Most of them pull it out or spray it every chance they get. We continue to pave and develop and otherwise subjugate our wild places. Last year's way station for migrating monarchs might this year be a condo or a subdivision or a highway cloverleaf.

And then, of course, there's climate change. New weather patterns mean different seasons for the wildflowers on which the monarchs depend for nectar. They also mean more weather extremes—storms, heat waves, cold snaps.

Worst of all is what's happening to the Mexican forests where the monarchs spend their winters.

They're disappearing. Some years ago, the president of Mexico declared with great hoopla and fanfare that his government would protect the monarchs. He turned about 160,000 hectares into a butterfly sanctuary.

It was a publicity stunt. In the past twenty-five years, more than half of the sanctuary has been cut down by illegal loggers.

So is the monarch doomed? No. Threatened for sure, but not doomed. This flimsiest of creatures, possessing the weight and fragility of a city bus transfer, has been criss-crossing our continent for eons against incalculable odds. The monarch is used to facing long odds and beating them.

This is one bimbo lightweight you don't want to bet against.

CRY ME A RIVER

I wish I had a river
I could skate away on.

—JONI MITCHELL

B ig deal. I grew up beside a river you could skate away on any day of the week, providing it was cold enough. It was called the Don River and it percolated down from the Oak Ridges Moraine through the clay flats of Southern Ontario, right through the belly of Hogtown until it finally ran into Lake Ontario.

Well, sort of ran. Truth is, skating was about all the Don River was good for when I was a kid. Each spring when the ice melted, the Don turned into a fetid sludge of toxic chemicals, agricultural runoff and human sewage that destroyed every living thing it touched. There were no fish or frogs or even tadpoles in my Don River. The odd rat slithering along its blistered banks, maybe. As kids we were forbidden to even wet our gumboots in the Don. It was one of the most polluted rivers in all of North America—so bad that in 1969 environmental groups staged a public funeral for the entire river system.

What's sadder is that the stalwart Ontario stewards of the

land who poisoned the Don were simply ahead of their time. People who live beside rivers around the world have followed their trailblazing lead. World Wildlife International recently published a list of the ten most threatened rivers on the planet. The list includes some of the most famous: the Yangtze, the Nile, the Ganges, the Rio Grande and the Blue Danube.

Which is a sick joke. The Danube that Johann Strauss immortalized a century and a half ago hasn't been blue for a long time. In fact it hasn't been a real river for a long time. More like a throughway. And a drainage ditch. And a latrine.

Eleven countries abut the Danube on its meandering three-thousand-kilometre journey to the Black Sea. It starts out pristine, sparkling and drinkable high in the Swiss Alps. It finishes its run as a grey-brown radioactive ooze of sewage, fertilizers and industrial waste so toxic it has all but destroyed the entire ecosystem of the Black Sea itself.

The Danube didn't go down without a fight. As late as the 1970s Hungarians were hauling two-metre sturgeon out of the Danube waters—with such regularity that they grew bored with their steady diet of caviar.

The sturgeon that didn't succumb to pollution were finally stopped by a massive hydroelectric dam constructed by the Soviets in 1973. From then on, any surviving sturgeon were physically prevented from returning to their spawning beds.

Bizarre. Someday some future race is going to construct a psychological profile of *Homo sapiens*, and I suspect they will be buffaloed by this psychotic anomaly: we made our homes and towns and cities beside our rivers for obvious reasons. They were our highways, our source of life and food and of our very essence—water.

And we systematically poisoned them, all over the world.

So is it all over for the Blue Danube? It's a near thing, but perhaps not. The countries that share the Danube now belong to the European Union, and the EU has very strict environmental

27

regulations. Every country admitted to the EU must adopt comprehensive environmental controls and policies.

And it's working. Concentrations of nitrogen in the river have dropped by 50 percent in the past twenty years. Phosphorus is down by 20 percent. For the first time in over a century, the waters of the Danube are getting cleaner.

And once more they have a model to follow.

Ontario's Don River.

Those Canuck environmental groups may have symbolically buried the Don back in 1969, but they didn't desert it. Over the following decades they badgered politicians to curb agricultural runoff and update sewer systems. They sponsored cleanup bees where volunteers pulled out the old tires, batteries, shopping carts and other junk that littered the riverbed. They also planted over ten thousand dogwood, highbush cranberry, white cedar, silver maple and other trees along the banks of the Don.

Not long ago Phil Goodwin, chairman of the East Don Parkland Partners and member of the Don Watershed Regeneration Council, had his own watershed moment.

Goodwin was standing on the banks of the Don about twenty kilometres upstream from its mouth. He looked down in the shallows and he beheld, slogging against the current, a dogged Chinook salmon battling its way upstream.

That's a sight that no one has seen since long before I was born—and I'm a greybeard.

Hey. If we can put salmon back in the Don, we can put Blue back in the Danube.

LAUGHING ALL THE WAY
TO THE GAS PUMP

Saw Kate getting out of her car downtown the other day. She took one look at me and erupted in a long, ululating belly laugh. I'm used to it. I know what it's about. Her guy rides a huge Ducati Testastretta S4S, a motorcycle the size of a black rhino.

Whereas I was on my new motor scooter.

I bought one of those 49 cc step-through jobbies. They're still relatively rare in Canada, but common as crabgrass in Europe. Near as I can make out, motor scooters are the vehicle of choice in London, Paris and pretty much all of Spain and Italy. Teenagers ride them to school. Lovers double up on them for dates. Everybody rides them: accountants and housewives, bank robbers and secretaries. In Granada I watched three nuns merrily billowing along in triplicate.

In Canada, however, scooters still have some distance to go in terms of public acceptance. I believe it's mostly an image problem.

First time my pal Jan saw my new set of wheels, he looked at me solemnly and said, "You realize you're never going to look cool on this thing."

I told him I'm in my sixties; I don't have to worry about cool anymore.

That said, Jan and Kate do share a point. On this side of the water, anything with two wheels and a motor is expected to give off a tantalizing whiff of outlaw. North Americans were weaned on motorcycle images from films like *Easy Rider* and *The Wild Ones*. Movies that featured shiny, menacing machines bestrode by über-macho studs like Fonda and Hopper, Marvin and Brando. They looked like mechanized Cossacks. It's hard to achieve that look on a dinky two-wheeler that comes in pastel colours and has to be going downhill to hit sixty kilometres an hour. Besides, you don't bestride a scooter. You perch on it, like somebody sipping a soy macchiato on a stool at Starbucks.

And I have to allow that those big Harleys, BMWs and Kawasakis have scooters whipped in the aural department as well. Listening to a full-bore motorcycle growl as it runs through the gears—rrrrrrrrrRRRRRRRNNNNN KA-CHUNG! rrrrrrrRRRRRRRRRNNNNNNNN KA-CHUNG!—is like hearing James Earl Jones denounce a Mississippi racist—all *basso profundo* rumbling and roaring.

Motor scooters don't even have gears. The transmission is automatic. To go forward, you simply twist the right handgrip. The keening whine that comes out of the engine when you crank that throttle sounds like a vacuum cleaner on helium.

There are other downsides to a scooter. You'd be foolish to take it out on a superhighway. You wouldn't want to be caught on one in a blizzard. And unless he's a chihuahua on Prozac, taking the family mutt for a spin is pretty much out.

But damn, they're fun. Swooping up and down roads and lanes, feeling the wind in your face, leaning into a curve, dipsydoodling around potholes and expired squirrels. I remember as a teenager driving the old man's car by myself for the first time.

That's the last time I had this much fun driving anything.

Getting behind the wheel isn't much fun anymore. Hasn't been for a long time. Driving nowadays is traffic gridlock and magenta-faced road sharers giving you the finger. It's radar guns and parking tickets. When I'm in my car, I spend way too much of my life either trapped behind some dithering doofus crawling along in first gear, or worrying about the methed-out mutt in the Trans Am who's crawling up my tailpipe.

On a scooter you don't have to worry so much about that stuff. You don't have to fret about parking either. Our towns and cities are still full of nooks and crannies more than big enough to accommodate a scooter. Usually I just slip mine in sideways between two parked cars. That way I only need about four feet of space, not twenty.

None of which addresses the image problem, but then it isn't the scooter that has the image problem, is it? It's the rider. Guys, all I can say is, if you're a little shaky about your masculinity or if your idea of a great night out is trolling for biker babes, then you're right; a scooter is not for you. Get yourself a chopper and one of those pee-pot helmets the bad biker dudes wear. Then hope that your bike doesn't fall over at an intersection some day and you have to pay some high school kids to help you get it up.

So to speak.

Me? I realize it'll be quilting night at the Hells Angels clubhouse before any biker babes flash me some thigh as I go putt-putting by, but you know what? I don't care. I'm having far too much fun. I was going to tell Kate that when I ran into her again down at the Shell station yesterday, but I changed my mind. She looked a little grumpy.

Don't blame her. Kate drives an SUV and she was filling her

tank at the time. I could hear an awful lot of bing-bing-bings as the pump recorded the damage.

Eighty-five . . . ninety . . . ninety-five bucks.

I was at the next pump, gassing up my scooter.

My fill-up? Four dollars and change—and that's from vapours to brim-full. Should last me about five days.

I decided against an ululating belly laugh. Wouldn't have sounded manly.

HERE'S MUD IN YOUR MOUTH

You'll eat a peck of dirt before you die.
—RUBY F. (MUM) BLACK, 1910–91

That would be my mother. The saying would be, in fact, one of my mother's favourite, if more inscrutable, catchphrases. She used it on me whenever I whined about the topsoil that clung to tasty carrots yanked from our garden. She uttered it whenever I kvetched about being expected to finish a cookie, notwithstanding the fact that she'd dropped it on the floor. Mum sported a cavalier, laissez-faire attitude toward everyday grit and grime that would horrify Martha Stewart and give a modern hygienist a dose of the vapours.

It scared me too—particularly when I discovered how big a peck was. My own mother was telling me that I could expect to eat a quarter of a bushel of filth in my lifetime? That's like four heaping cereal bowls! What the hell kind of a world was this she'd brought me into?

Answer: a very fecund one. Common dirt is not filth, of course, even though we're encouraged to regard it as such almost from birth. ("Oh, Billy! Look at your hands, they're disgusting! Get into the bathroom and wash them right now!")

Turns out Billy's hands aren't so much filthy as teeming with life. According to Graham Harvey, author of a book called *We Want Real Food*, one teaspoonful of healthy soil contains more than five billion organisms from some ten thousand different species.

And it's not poison. If it was, every human being with a condition known as pica would be dead as a doornail. Pica? An overpowering compulsion to ingest non-edible items, particularly dirt, clay, pebbles and even cigarette ash. The name for the condition comes from the Latin name for magpie, a bird renowned for eating just about anything.

Estimates are vague as to how many people have this gastronomic itch, but it is not unknown among mothers-to-be. Many pregnant women eat way more than a peck of dirt while they're carrying children. Pica also affects youngsters, particularly in impoverished areas.

Nobody knows why the condition arises, but it's a safe bet that Pica-prone folks are seeking some kind of nutritional benefit they're not getting from their regular diets.

Perhaps more of us will be looking to dirt for sustenance soon. According to author Harvey, ordinary vegetables where he lives (Britain) have lost more than a quarter of their magnesium and iron content and nearly half of their calcium over the past half-century. The result, he claims, is a bland harvest of insipid, watered-down food stocks, which leads to malnourished animals—including humans—and a whole litany of diseases and ailments affecting us all. We still need all the vitamins and minerals our caveman forebears did, he says.

We're just not getting them.

Which may help explain an unusual medical experiment Down Under. Researchers at the University of Western Australia dosed a select group of asthmatic children with a special pill that they hoped would eliminate the symptoms of their disease. The kids in the control group received a specific daily medication that included a mixture of various strains of probiotic bacteria and antioxidants.

Or to put it plainly, the kids each got a dirt pill a day.

The researchers hoped the bacteria in the dirt pill will replicate common germs that all children are—or used to be—exposed to during their first years of life. Their theory is that these asthmatic children did not receive a sufficient quantity of bacteria-laden dirt in their early years to develop physiological immunity. The researchers believe that the children's asthmatic condition is merely an allergic reaction to their inadequate diet.

If the researchers are correct, the experiment will prove that all those asthmatic kids need is a bit more common, everyday, run-of-the-schoolyard dirt in their bellies.

Maybe even a peck's worth.

Good old Mum. Just slightly ahead of her time.

NO BUTTS ABOUT IT

*You know what bugs me? People who smoke in
restaurants. That's why I always carry a water
pistol filled with gasoline.*

—PAUL PROVENZA

Poor old long-suffering nicotine addicts. On the run again.
In my section of The Great White North, puffers have
been informed that under a new law, they can have a smoke
break or a coffee break, but they can't have both. Not at the
same time in the same place anyway. They can sit down and
light up a cigarette or they can sit down and suck back a Tim
Hortons double-double. But their smoking oasis and their
coffee-klatching centre must be at least twenty-five metres apart.
Which could lead to the absurd sight of some schlub lighting up
an Export A, taking a drag, then sprinting across the patio to sit
at another table and sip some coffee, then galloping back to the
table with the ashtray to . . . well, you get the picture.

So Kafkaesque. And such a far cry from the world I grew
up in. Back in the Fuming Fifties and Smoky Sixties, we smoked
everywhere all the time. We lit up in cars, in offices, in living
rooms and in airplanes. I remember once being in a conference

room with twenty other people for a day-long gab about some corporate thing or other. At the end of the morning session, one woman stood up and nervously asked if, for the afternoon, it would be possible for the smokers to abstain or at least step outside to indulge their habit out of consideration for the non-smokers in the group.

We tar-stained wretches looked at her like she'd just descended from Mars.

Smokers ruled. But that was then, and this is now. A recent survey reveals that three out of four American households now forbid anyone to smoke in their home. I haven't seen comparable statistics for Canada, but I have to think that in the ever polite, politically correct envirobubble that envelops our country, the percentage is at least as high and probably higher. What I know for sure is that it's getting increasingly difficult in Canada to find a public place where you can eat your dinner and fire up a gasper at the same time.

And frankly I'm all for that. Number one: I'm an ex-smoker. That makes me automatically sanctimonious and socially insufferable on the topic of my former habit. Number two: I want my restaurants back. In the last anti-smoking offensive, addicts were banished to outside patios and covered terraces to indulge their craving. It was a pyrrhic victory for non-smokers. We won the battle but lost the war. What happened was that we, the pink-of-lung and obedient, were consigned to the dank and dismal restaurant interior while smokers got the primo turf outside under the trees. We could join them out there if we chose, of course, but it meant we would be inhaling second-hand carcinogens and would smell like a poolroom when we got home.

Well, no more. Non-smokers can once more sit in the open air (weather permitting) and inhale only car, bus and industrial fumes as is our God-given inalienable right. Smokers are—quelle surprise—ticked off, but they just don't get it. They see being banished from the company of non-smokers as an infringement on their rights.

Listen, folks. We don't care if you smoke. We don't care if you inhale whole burning hay bales. We just don't want you to smoke around us. The comedian Steve Martin said it best. When someone asked him, "Do you mind if I smoke?" he smiled genially and said, "Not at all. Do you mind if I fart?"

That said, it may be time to rein in the anti-smoking zealots just a hair. I see that the Motion Picture Association of America is now considering a new restriction for movies. Not only will films be classified according to their depictions of sex, violence, and adult language, they will also be judged for "glamorizing smoking."

So let me see now . . . how would that work? Children would still see people smoking every day—at the bus stop, down by the corner store, in front of the high school—but they'd be protected from seeing Humphrey Bogart in *Casablanca*?

Bad idea. Listen. Everybody in the world now knows that smoking isn't glamorous; it's stupid. I've yet to meet a smoker who doesn't—in his or her heart of hearts—want to dump the habit.

What people who have never smoked don't know is that giving it up is damn hard. Everett Koop, the former US Surgeon General, said that nicotine addiction is as strong as heroin addiction, just a little cheaper.

And is there anybody left on the planet who still believes smoking is harmless? If there is, that person is in serious denial. As comedian Dennis Miller says, if you're saying you didn't know cigarettes were bad for you, you're lying through that hole in your trachea.

PAPER? PLASTIC? OR HERMÈS?

Everything is simpler than you think. And more complex than you can imagine.

—GOETHE

Not to put myself on the same cerebral plane as Herr Goethe or anything, but I've noticed that myself. How nothing is really simple, I mean. Take a three-word question that gets asked a gazillion times a day at checkout counters around the world:

"Paper or plastic?"

When first confronted with this choice many years ago, I blurted, "Paper, please," and felt very virtuous, knowing that at least one environmentally sensitive citizen wouldn't be contributing to the landfill problem of non-degrading plastic bags.

I basked happily in the warmth of self-congratulation for some time, until some ecozealot pointed out that more air and water gets polluted in the production of paper than in the production of plastic bags. And besides, you can use a plastic bag over and over again. Don't try that trick with the paper bag full of damp celery you brought home.

So I set an empty pail in the cupboard under my sink and

began putting all my plastic grocery bags in there, hauling them out for reuse as needed. But taking advantage of the darkness of the cupboard, my plastic bags multiplied like mayflies and were soon spilling out on the kitchen floor.

And even the ones I reused had a short life. Sooner or later they split or ripped and had to be tossed in the garbage, eventually to make their way to a landfill site where, I was assured with a sniff, they would take approximately ten centuries to break down.

There is, of course, a solution to the shopper's paper-or-plastic dilemma. It's called the BYODB option. Stands for Bring Your Own Damned Bags. This is something Europeans figured out decades ago. If you stand at the checkout counter at a Tesco or Sainsbury's in England waiting for the clerk to bag your purchases, they'll look at you as if you're daft. "Didn't bring bags?" they'll ask incredulously. Then they'll hand you some, but you'll pay for every bag you get. European shoppers go to the grocery store with cloth or mesh bags tucked under their arms as a matter of course.

It's something that's slowly catching on over here. Superstore now charges for every plastic bag it gives you. An increasing number of shoppers are taking the hint and bringing in their own cloth bags. It's an idea you'd think even North Americans couldn't screw up.

You'd be wrong.

The good news: we consumers are gradually cottoning on to the idea of bringing our own cotton bags. The bad news: Paris Hilton is in charge of the advertising campaign.

Might as well be. The latest must-have fashion accessory? Designer shopping bags. Some of these cloth bags are relatively cheap. Mountain Equipment Co-op sells a bag for $9.99. The Roots Eco Bag will set you back $14.95.

But that's low-end stuff, strictly for the lumpenproletariat. No, if you really want to be a trendy, champion-of-the-environment

Beautiful Person, you need to pick up the I Am Not a Plastic Bag tote from British designer Anya Hindmarch. This bag originally cost about twenty bucks Canadian, but it sold out and has since become a collector's item. Online eBay shopper wannabes pay up to 150 dollars for one of these bags.

And that's still pretty plebian. If you really want to make yourself a contender for the Bono-Suzuki Good Housekeeping Seal of Approval, I think you're looking at The Stella McCartney organic canvas bag. It's only four ninety-five.

That's four hundred and ninety-five. Dollars.

It gets sillier. Castiglioni offers a foldable grocery bag for $843—and to add insult to obscenity, it's nylon. But if you really want to go top-drawer, pick yourself up a Silky Pop bag with the famous Hermès logo plastered all over it.

Price tag for this cutie? US$960.

We're talking shopping bags here. No zippers, no buttons, no secret compartments. No fine, hand-tooled Italian leather. Just cotton-pickin' cotton bags.

It's all about advertising, of course. Every designer bag carries the company logo prominently displayed. Will Rogers once defined advertising as "the art of convincing people to spend money they don't have on something they don't need."

Modern merchandisers have taken that equation to a new plateau.

Now they want to sell us a bag to take it home in.

TAKE A HİKE, EH?

Psst—wanna get in shape? Have I got a program for you.

Forget your thlons, bia- and tria-, and marathons. Don't batter your MasterCard with big-ticket items like downhill skis, cross-country mountain bikes, windsurfers, scuba tanks or paragliders. Leave the barbells on the rack, the medicine balls in the closet. Let your Curves membership lapse. Never darken the sweaty portals of your local gym again.

The program I'm flogging requires no fees, no specialized equipment and no brain-clotting timetables or schedules. You practise where you want, when you want, indoors or outdoors and as laid-back or gut-busting as you please. I can virtually guarantee you will pull no hamstrings, pop no groins, sprain no ligaments and pinch no nerves. It's a carcass-friendly pastime, is my program.

And if you, like me, are somewhat silhouettically challenged—no worries. My exercise regime is totally spandex- and Lycra-free.

It's called walking.

Actually I may have fudged a bit on the "no special equipment required." If you insist on spending money on walking accessories, our multi-billion-dollar sports gear industry will be more than pleased to separate you from a significant chunk of your disposable income. There are Nordic walking poles. There are stout Friar-Tuckian walking staffs with embedded compasses. Your local shoe store can show you an entire wall devoted to walking shoes. Odd, that a skill most of us master while we're still barefoot and wearing diapers would give rise to such a plethora of specialized gear.

'Tis all shuck and jive, folks. When it comes to walking, pretty much any shoe will do.

And it's not just a cheap and pleasant way to firm up muscle and get your cardiovascular system firing on all cylinders, walking is a healthy substitute for those happy pills as well. Researchers at the University of Essex in England recently treated a group of twenty patients suffering from depression. They prescribed no pills or pep talks, just a thirty-minute walk in the park. Following the walk, the patients were debriefed. Seventy-one percent said that after the walk they felt less depressed; 90 percent said they felt generally better about themselves.

Walking's not just a psychological pick-me-up. It can literally save your life. Another study conducted by researchers at the University of Pittsburgh and published in the journal of the American Medical Association came up with a blunt rule of thumb for those of us of a certain age: if you can't walk four hundred metres today, chances are you won't be alive in six years. Dr. Anne Newman, lead author of the study, said, "We found that the people who could not complete the walk were at an extremely high risk of later disability and death."

What's even more ominous is that all the people—2,700 men and women aged seventy to seventy-nine—believed they could walk four hundred metres. A lot of them found out they couldn't. "What was really surprising," says Dr. Newman, "is that these people were not aware of how limited they actually were."

My final pitch for walking? It could halt climate change. Okay, not halt, maybe, but at least give it a significant whack across the shins. Consider this: every single footstep you and I take generates six to eight watts of kinetic energy. Now consider that there are nearly seven billion of us hairless bipeds on this planet, each of us pumping out, say, seven watts every time we take a step. Imagine if all that energy could be harvested.

How? Researchers have already created a prototype generator, capable of turning kinetic energy into electrical current, and it's small enough to be embedded in footwear.

A British firm called Facility Architects is thinking even bigger. Their scientists are developing sensors capable of harvesting all kinds of vibrational energy from train stations, factories, bridges, trestles, anything that trembles with energy generated by traffic, heavy machinery or simply plodding pedestrians. Researchers estimate that such sensors could save two hundred billion dollars a year in the US alone.

And shall I tell you about the most beautiful walk I ever took? It was a nightwalk, a relatively new fad that you really should try sometime. You have to choose your terrain, of course—I wouldn't try a nightwalk in heavy bush or around the rim of Kakabeka Falls—but walking in the dark without flashlights, without any strobing headlights or urban glow on the horizon, really is a rare and transcending experience. Your eyes are no longer reliable, so your other senses step up to the plate. Your feet mold themselves to the earth beneath you. You are aware of the slightest breeze on your skin. You hear sounds and smell scents you wouldn't normally have noticed. You really feel like you are part of the landscape, part of the night.

My nightwalk took place on Paradise Island in the Bahamas. A group of us rose before dawn and walked along the beach in silence, in darkness, to a long cement jetty. There we sat, legs dangling, looking across the ocean in the direction of Africa, watching the sky turn from the blackest black through greys to the lightest of blues.

And then we watched the sun come up.

No one said a word. There were no words to say.

MAKING A DIFFERENCE, A STARFISH AT A TIME

The year: 1967. The setting: a small town in the Atlas Mountains of Morocco.

I was a young Canadian hitchhiker and I was broke. Very. I had a couple of traveller's cheques in my jeans, but the villagers wouldn't know a traveller's cheque from a hockey puck, and the Fast of Ramadan was on. The only bank in town had been closed for three days and looked to stay shut for at least another twenty-four hours. I was down to my last Moroccan dirham, which meant I didn't have enough cash to make a phone call, much less order a proper meal.

Oh yeah . . . I was also hungry. Very.

I tracked down the cheapest, nastiest hole-in-the-wall café I could find, ascertained that I had just enough money for a bowl of the soup of the day, then joined a chain of ragged, slightly sinister-looking Arabs, all clad in djellabas. I arrived at the soup cauldron at exactly the same moment as another customer, a hooded Moroccan of whose face all I could see was a pair of glowering eyes over a hawk nose over a bushy moustache.

Unaccountably—for I was very hungry and not given to excessive displays of politeness—I gestured for him to go ahead of me. Without a word of thanks or acknowledgement, he swept in front of The Infidel, got his bowl of soup, paid and disappeared out the door.

After I was served I reached into my pocket to pay with my last bit of cash. The server waved me off. "*C'est bon*," he said. My soup had been paid for.

By the surly, uncommunicative, sinister-looking Moroccan stranger whom I never saw again.

It was only a passing gesture worth maybe fifteen or twenty cents, but I haven't forgotten it in forty years. I like to think that random act of kindness mellowed me some, perhaps even made me a bit less of a jerk than I might have turned out to be.

Random acts of kindness are like that—sort of spiritual Canada Savings Bonds that pay off premiums, unexpected and surprisingly rich, way down the road.

Let's face it: you and I personally are not going to solve global warming, eradicate AIDS, or set up a peace dove shuttle service between Israel and Palestine. The world is full of huge, intractable problems that bedevil far finer minds than ours. But it is also speckled with moments, openings and opportunities to make some small improvement in someone else's life.

Take the Coffee Angel.

This is a woman, a divorced mother of two, who lives in Toronto and likes her coffee double-double with milk, not cream.

That is all we know about her. That is about as much as we will ever know. But one day, should you happen to be in a Tim Hortons Drive-Thru, you might cruise up to the takeout window, pick up your order, and be told by the Tim Hortons cashier, "That's okay, it's been paid for."

By the Coffee Angel.

It's what she does. She drives up to the takeout window, places her order for a double-double with milk, motions with her head to the vehicle behind her and tells the cashier quietly, "I'll pay for whatever they're having too." And she does. Whether it's just coffee, a sandwich, a bowl of soup or all three. Then she drives away. She repeats the exercise at irregular intervals at Tim Hortons Drive-Thrus throughout the city.

An enterprising *Globe and Mail* reporter tracked her down and asked her why. "Because it feels so good," she says, "to do something nice for someone else."

Does she think it makes a difference?

"Hopefully it shocks them," she says. "Hopefully it injects some positive energy into their day so they can feel better about themselves. I know my kids and I sure do."

Not surprisingly, they love her at Tim Hortons. "She brightens all our days," says one employee. "Sometimes she even starts a chain reaction, with as many as five cars buying in succession for all the people behind them."

Does she make a difference? Reminds me of the story of the cynic who came across a simple soul, wandering along the seashore, throwing starfish stranded by the outgoing tide back into the water. The cynic snorted. Oil slicks, sewage outfalls, unchecked pollution from a thousand different sources and here is one man on one beach in the whole world, saving starfish one at a time.

"Do you think," he sneered at the simple soul, "that what you're doing makes any difference?"

And the simple soul replied, "It does to the starfish."

WELCOME TO EARTH

A DREAM VACATiON? DON'T FOLLOW ME

They closed Haleakala National Park on the Hawaiian island of Maui recently. Too much snow. The newspapers carried photos of kids clumping together their very first clumsy snowmen in the Haleakala parking lot. One local dad was snapped avidly shovelling snow into a picnic cooler. Said he was going to take the stuff to his daughter's pre-school class "to show the students what this stuff is like."

The Hawaiians were enthralled, amazed, mesmerized. As a visiting hoarfrost-hardened Canuck, I was merely bemused. Here I was in a tropical Garden of Eden, when my biggest problems should have been choosing between snorkelling or hammocking, jumbo prawns on the patio or lining up for luau tickets under the palms. But no, they were closing parks and issuing severe weather alerts because it was snowing in Hawaii.

And I thought, of course it's snowing in Hawaii—I'm here.

But perhaps we haven't been introduced? Hello, my name is Arthur. I am the Darth Vader of Vacationing. The Hellspawn of Holidays. The Typhoid Mary of Tourism. Wherever I choose to spend my sabbaticals, you can rest assured that the winds will wrack, the heavens will weep and old Mr. Sun will be a dedicated no-show.

It's a hands-down, lead-pipe given. Two winters ago I flew to the southern tip of the Iberian Peninsula in order to spend two weeks on the Costa del Sol. That's Spanish for "the sunny coast," and it's not just a cliché. There are cheery, multilingual roadside signs welcoming you to "the warmest winter destination in all of Europe."

And well it may be—when I'm not there. During my fortnight, an Arctic-class wind lifted picturesque tiles off the roofs of picturesque Spanish *casas* and smashed them on the ice-glazed, picturesque streets below. The rain came in like machine-gun fire from the bleak grey Mediterranean, tattooing our windows until I thought the panes would shatter. The colourful local marketplaces were deserted. The bulls in the *plaza de toros* fled to Mexico for the winter. The flamenco dancers wore mittens.

Mind you, it didn't rain and blow for the entire two weeks. A couple of days were merely overcast.

I should have known better. A few years back I took my sweetie for a winter vacation to the Canary Islands. What could go wrong? The Canaries are off the coast of freakin' Africa— practically on the equator, for crying out loud. "You'll love it," I crooned. "It's desert country. Palm trees. Cactuses. Blazing sunshine dawn till dusk."

All true, until Yours Truly cleared customs. During our two weeks it was so frigid even the hardy German and Danish women tourists declined to go topless. And so wet that the *ministerio de turismo* was reduced to issuing flood warnings and road washout alerts.

I will never forget the defining moment of that trip. We were in a taxi, my increasingly tight-lipped sweetie and I, sloshing through the sodden streets of Las Palmas. As the overburdened wipers strained to deflect the deluge pouring down on the wind-shield, the taxi driver was earnestly assuring us that *"nunca"*—never—*"en veinte-cinco años"*—in twenty-five years—had the Canary Islands been buffeted by monsoons like this.

Oddly this failed to thrill us as much as it did the driver.

I hate to go all superstitious, but I think it's pretty obvious that the weather gods have it in for me. You'd think I'd have learned that by now. After all I've been tornadoed in Texas, deluged in Delhi, flooded in Florida, swamped in Swaziland and involuntarily inundated in Indonesia.

Mexico? Don't speak to me of Mexico. I've been to Mexico and back, trailing hailstorms, whiteouts, cyclones and torrential downpours in my wallowing wake. I've had the same effect on Colorado, Arizona, Louisiana and New Mexico.

My talent for attracting bad vacation weather became so unnerving that last year I decided to save myself a wallet full of money and an ice chest of grief. When winter vacation time rolled around, I passed. I decided to stay in Canada for the duration.

Remember what a crummy winter we had last year? Mea culpa. My fault, folks. Sorry about that.

Next winter? Well, I hear wonderful things about south Queensland in Australia. It's officially tropical. The Aussie tourist propaganda refers to it as the Sunshine State. More to the point, it took the title for hottest place on earth one day a couple of years back—69.3°C. That's a mercury-popping 156.7 degrees on the old Fahrenheit scale.

Sounds good to me. That's where I'm headed next January.

You might want to consider cornering the Queensland umbrella and ear muff market before the stampede.

iF KEVLAR'S COOL,
A SWEATER'S BETTER

Breaking news, gentlemen. One day soon, you and I will be able to rise of a morn, throw on our shirts for the day and immediately smell like a strawberry.

Or an orange, or a lemon, or mint—or even a double-shot espresso.

This fashion breakthrough is the brainchild of Tessitura Tainia, a Milanese textile manufacturing company. A spokesman for the company explains that "the concept is to make a shirt that is not only an element for dressing but also of distinction."

You've got us there, Tessitura Tainia spokesman. Few apparel statements are more distinctive than arriving at a cocktail party smelling like a giant Sunkist orange.

But the fruit-flavoured chemise is hardly the only fashionista assault on the male torso these days. Consider the twenty-nine-pocket travel vest, machine-washable, in black or khaki, now available from the US retailer Hammacher-Schlemmer.

Twenty-nine pockets. "Ergonomically designed" pockets,

my catalogue assures me. Some have zippers, others have magnetic closures. Two of the deeper pockets contain elastic loops for those oh-so-crucial water bottles one mustn't try to traverse a shopping mall without. Plus the vest is wired for sound. There's a "patented cord management system" networked throughout the vest that allows the wearer to connect ear buds to an iPod or MP3 player or that vintage Klingon decoder ring.

With all due respect to Hammacher-Schlemmer, this is not a vest; it's an ecosystem.

Understand that I speak as a vest guy. I wear a vest most of the time I'm vertical. My vest is my purse, my backpack and my glove compartment. In it I carry reading specs, my wallet, a notebook, my car keys, a pair of sunglasses, and if it's not too bulky, any book I happen to be reading at the time.

That's the great thing about vests—you can load 'em up like ocean-going bulk carriers with all the crap you think you could possibly need for the day.

Which is also the horrible thing about vests—because they can add 20 percent to your body weight, give you severe neck sprain, make you look like the Michelin Man and drive you crazy trying to figure out which pocket you put that chocolate bar in. My vest has seven pockets, which I figure is about four too many.

Oh well. At least my vest isn't bulletproof. That would be an option if I was outfitting my kids for school in the Boston area this year: bulletproof Kevlar backpacks for school kids. They're selling like hotcakes at 175 bucks a pop.

Or I could just fit the nippers out with a GPS jacket. That choice is a little pricier—a British company called Bladerunner is selling children's jackets (also Kevlar-lined) with embedded global tracking systems for about five hundred dollars each (plus a twenty-dollar-a-month satellite linkup charge). Imagine—a kid's coat that shows up on radar. Its built-in tracking system allows you to keep tabs on the little beggars wherever they go.

At least until they take off the jacket and leave it by the sandbox.

When did covering our backs get so complicated? We got along fine for several millennia ripping off whichever animal hide we could steal when said animal wasn't paying attention. We moved up through grass weaves, then wool, cotton, linen and the various "lons"—ny-, ban- and or-. Now this—web-savvy windbreakers.

There is, I'm happy to report, a much simpler, more beautiful solution to the male torso coverage problem and it's made right here in Canada, exclusively on Vancouver Island.

It's called the Cowichan sweater, an artistic melding of sheep's wool and native designs hand-knitted by the women of First Nations bands in the Cowichan Valley. That's it. No microweave miracle fibres, no add-ons, Velcro tabs or brass buckles. Just natural wool and native craft. And the ladies know what they're doing. They're keeping alive a tradition that goes back 150 years.

The classic Cowichan sweater comes in two colour combinations: black (shades of brown, really) and white; or if you prefer, white and black. It is warm, waterproof, exquisitely beautiful and all the coat you'll probably ever need. And virtually indestructible. Owners leave them in their wills to their grandkids.

Think your grandchildren will be wearing your Tommy Hilfiger windbreaker a generation or so from now?

And the Cowichan sweater is world-famous. Bing Crosby wore his proudly. So did Pierre Trudeau and John George Diefenbaker. Not to mention the world's two most famous Elizabeths, Taylor and Windsor.

Good enough for politicians as various as Trudeau and the Queen? Good enough for me.

BOYS' NIGHT OUT—
NO GIRLS ALLOWED

Ever wondered why it seems like only women belong to book clubs?

So did we. That's why we started up MOBCOSSI.

That would stand for Men's Only Book Club on Salt Spring Island.

The "we" would stand for John, John, Jan, Stan, Harry, Andrew, Alex, Derek *et moi*. Which is to say two farmers, two writers, one ex-physics prof turned hippie-musician, a Hollywood voice-over actor, a bookseller and a world-class expert on Persian carpets.

Hey. It's Salt Spring.

Oh yeah—I forgot to mention the ex-air traffic controller from East Timor who may or may not now be working in Kabul. Or Dubai. Or Belgium. He pops in, too, when he's in town.

We thought that it would be dead easy running a book club for men only. We would meet once a month, take turns choosing one of our favourite books and then—you know—like . . . talk about it. How hard could it be?

Turns out, pretty hard. The first hurdle was the date for the monthly meeting. Most of us thought the first Wednesday of each month would work, but then Harry mentioned that his Celtic band gets together every other Wednesday, so we switched to Thursday. But then somebody (the air traffic guy, I think) said the second Thursday of the month would work better for him, so we batted that around for a while.

We've been getting together for three years now, and what's firmly established is that we meet on some Thursday. As each month winds down, we bombard the ether with flurries of nervous emails—*Is it this Thursday or what? Jan*—And then, of course, following the meeting attended by half the roster, another fusillade of emails—*I thot we agreed second Thursday! John.*

Date confusion is the least significant of a mare's nest of misunderstandings, misconceptions, puzzles and conundrums that plague MOBCOSSI. Take book selection. We try to stay one book ahead, which is to say that at the end of each meeting, we choose the book for the next month and for the month following that.

Naturally, when book club night rolls around at least half the attendees who show up have read the wrong book. "I'm positive we said *Kitchen Confidential* for March and *Microserfs* for April." (Alex) "Other way around, doofus." (Harry)

That's still considered a successful MOBCOSSI meeting based on the fact that (a) some members showed up and (b) they read something. We have a clause in the MOBCOSSI constitution stipulating that it's unnecessary for a member to have actually read the book in order to attend the book club meeting.

Our other big problem: I don't think we've quite finessed book club protocol. Maybe one of us should volunteer to watch Oprah and take notes. I talked to a woman friend who's in a book club, and she explained how her members get together and select books for the coming year. Then each club member chooses a book, reads it, takes notes, researches the author, prints out his or her bibliography, photocopies reviews of the book from the *Globe and Mail* and the *New York Times Review of Books*. At the meeting she presents the whole package to the book club along with a personally crafted mini-essay about what the book meant to her—and a list of suggested discussion points.

MOBCOSSI doesn't work like that. What happens at our meeting is, well, we have a round of beers, grumble about local politics, kid Stan about his hat and check out the hockey game on the TV over the bar. Finally somebody says, "Well, what about the book?" Somebody else says, "I liked it." Somebody else says, "I couldn't stand it." Somebody else says, "Are we talking about the Afghanistan book or the one where lizards take over the world?"

Occasionally we get almost trenchant. "I thought what he wrote about the train crash was really good." (Andrew) "Train crash? That was no train crash! That was . . . like . . . an extended metaphor for his nervous breakdown." (Alex) "Bullshit." (Harry).

And so on.

It's a bumpy, fractious ride, is a MOBCOSSI get-together, but I love it. I especially love it because it's my turn to choose a book this month. I've already picked it out. It's by a French author, Pierre Bayard, and it's called *How to Talk About Books You Haven't Read*.

Naturally I haven't read it, but I like the excerpt that appears on the back cover. "In my experience," writes the author, "it is totally possible to carry on an engaging conversation about a book you haven't read—including, and perhaps especially, with someone else who hasn't read it either . . . The point is not to be correct, but to have an opinion."

Well hell. *Terre* to Monsieur Bayard: MOBCOSSIANS have known that for years.

Truth is, Professor Bayard's book is not what the Men's Only Book Club on Salt Spring really needs. I can tell you what we need.

We need a mother.

FRONT PAGE CHALLENGE— IT'S BACK

Do you miss Pierre and Betty? The Foth? Webster and Sinc? The affable, dapper and ever unflappable Fred Davis? Well, good news: *Front Page Challenge* is back.

And for those callow, damp-behind-the-iPod-buds striplings out there who think *Front Page Challenge* must be another lame variation on so-called reality shows, let me fill you in. *Front Page Challenge* was an icon, an institution, a Gibraltar of Canadian television. Back in the summer of 1957 it swam through the ether and emerged on the black and white TV screens of Mr. and Mrs. Canada. It was an off-season replacement program, a slung together hash consisting of one mini-celeb (Toby Robins) and a clutch of Canadian print and radio journalists whose chore it was to identify the hidden mystery guest, and more importantly, the headline that made the guest worth hiding from view.

Critics panned it. Who wants to watch a herd of grizzled journos chasing down old news stories? But a funny thing happened on the way to the summer reruns bin. Turned out that the Canadian public loved the show. What made it work? Some weird alchemy galvanized the motley mix—curmudgeonly Gordon Sinclair, the eye-stopping Toby Robbins—most especially Pierre Berton with his black-button eyes and his fearsome and shark-like instinct for the journalistic jugular. The resultant brew was quintessential Canadiana—a weekly current events lesson wrapped in a neon boa of show biz razzmatazz. The *Beaver* magazine dubbed it "a quiz show for brainiacs."

Toby Robins was eventually replaced by the elegant, cerebral Betty Kennedy, and guest panelists came and went, but the nitty-gritty of the Berton-Sinclair-Kennedy nexus, ever shepherded by the urbane Fred Davis, endured to make the show a Canadian hit.

And what a hit it was. *Front Page Challenge* stayed on the air for thirty-eight years in the longest run of any CBC television show in history. It was Canada's first-ever (last-ever?) strut in big-time television, and the producers wrangled big-name guests aboard each week. Martin Luther King was a mystery guest on *Front Page Challenge*. So were Eleanor Roosevelt and Boris Karloff, Errol Flynn and Gordie Howe. Six Canadian prime ministers sat in that chair. Ah yes, those were the days, my friend . . .

And what was my point again? Oh right . . . that the CBC is bringing the show back to life. Not the original show of course; they couldn't. Most of the principals—Fred Davis, Toby Robins, Jack Webster, and Pierre Berton—are no longer with us. And it's unlikely that Betty Kennedy, now an octogenarian and a senator, could spare the time to be a panelist.

Nope, the CBC plans to bring back a rejuvenated, funked-up version of the old warhorse. This is not a rumour I heard down at Moe's Tavern, nor is it an internet hoax. I know it for a fact, because I know who's going to fill Fred Davis's natty Gucci loafers.

Me.

Well . . . maybe. The fact is, a while ago the CBC talent scouts fanned out across the country from coast to coast in search of a whole new lineup for a modern version of the show. They held auditions in CBC TV studios across the country. I strutted my stuff at the Vancouver studios one August afternoon along with six other hopefuls.

So is this gig in the bag for me? Will I soon be too busy jetting around the country to tend to my little cabbage patch of columns? Will I be swanning through the streets of Salt Spring Island in a limo with tinted windows, beating back the groupies with a riding crop?

Probably not.

Truth to tell, I caught the CBC audition team at the tail end of its cross-country swing. It had already listened to and filmed hundreds of panelist hopefuls and dozens of potential Fred Davis clones.

I think they were a little tired. Pretty much going through the paces for the sake of geographical correctness, as it were. Why the pessimism, Watson? Oh, little signs. Like no teleprompter. "Just read from the script," I was told. (Umm, no. Radio hosts are allowed to read from scripts. TV hosts are supposed to look at the camera and fake omniscience.)

There were other signs too—like cheap folding chairs for the mystery guests. A "studio audience" consisting of three or four strays plucked from the halls of the CBC. And the "complimentary gift" to each auditionee: a lime green T-shirt with "Radio-Canada" emblazoned on the front.

Guest hosts for the Oscars get Rolex watches, cashmere jackets and enough bling to open a jewelry franchise. CBC Television gives you an undershirt commemorating the French-language division of their radio service.

Bitter? Nah. It was a hoot being Fred Davis, if only for a day. And how many of us get to tread in the bootprints of Pierre

Berton, Jack Webster, Gordon Sinclair and other dead white Canadians?

Besides, I knew I'd at least get a column out of it.

Plus I'll always have the T-shirt.

CHRISTOPHER AND THE CHICKEN BONE

Forensically speaking, we live in fascinating times. If you don't believe me, catch any episode of *CSI: Miami* or *CSI: New York* or *CSI: . . .* does North Battleford have a franchise yet?

Sure, I know. Real criminal investigators scoff at the hype, the glitz and the comic book over-simplification of the crime scene investigation shows. At how brooding, besunglassed head honcho Horatio Caine manages to take a milligram of fifty-year-old ear wax from the sole of a ditchdigger's workboot and use it to identify, track down and collar a serial arsonist, all in an hour of TV time with pauses for commercials. Real crime investigations aren't like that, the experts say. Well, of course they aren't, but the leaps and strides made in forensics in just the past few years are pretty mind-boggling all the same.

Thanks to the miracle of DNA analysis, police now routinely reopen cold cases that have been mouldering on the shelf for decades. Just a few traces of DNA taken at the time of the crime can lead to the conviction—or exoneration—of crime suspects years after the event.

And it's not just murderers and burglars and bank robbers that have to look over their shoulders. DNA investigation is rewriting history. Consider the case of Christopher Columbus and the chicken bone.

What was that jingle we all learned in grade school? "In 1492, Columbus sailed the ocean blue . . ."

. . . and landed in the Caribbean, checked out the islands, subjugated the natives and looted the joint, which eventually led to more Europeans making the trip and, well, eventually, the settlement of a continent.

Columbus "discovered" the New World. Says so in the history books. (We will leave aside, for the moment, the hundreds of thousands of native North and South Americans already living here, blissfully unaware that they were lost.)

Yes, well. Thanks to some very recent forensic work, it looks like we're going to have to get ourselves some new history books.

Forensic scientists are all agog over the work done by Alice Storey, a Canadian anthropologist, whose work seems to indicate that Columbus didn't discover the New World at all—that no European did. The New World, the evidence seems to say, was discovered by Polynesians about a century before the *Niña*, the *Pinta* and the *Santa Maria* dropped anchor in the Caribbean.

Professor Storey's proof? A chicken bone—a very old chicken bone—unearthed on Chile's Arauco Peninsula, about four hundred kilometres south of Santiago.

Professor Storey specializes in molecular science. She managed to isolate the long-defunct chicken's DNA from the ancient bone and to match it to a breed of chicken found only in the Polynesian islands. Researchers had already established that the bone dated from sometime between AD 1321 and 1407. Ergo, this bird had been clucking around South America and wound up as somebody's dinner at least eighty-five years before Columbus and his buddies showed up—and it had come from Polynesia.

So, case closed. Polynesians, not Europeans, get the nod for "discovering" the new world, right?

But what's that nagging voice I keep hearing? Sounds . . . Scandinavian, sorta. Seems to be coming from the tip of that upraised peninsular finger of Newfoundland's rocky west coast.

Seems to be coming from a village called L'Anse aux Meadows.

That's where a Norwegian explorer and his archeologist wife discovered the remains of a Viking village back in 1960. A village that has been forensically dated to roughly the year AD 1000.

Which is to say there were Europeans wandering around the beaches of Newfoundland—and hence the Americas—at least four centuries before Polynesian chickens or Italian adventurers showed up.

Maybe the Vikings need to hire a PR firm. They were incontestably here first, but like some Nordic version of Rodney Dangerfield, they "can't get no respect."

Pity. There's a great story there. Some experts believe that the Vikings ran afoul of the First Nations people after they invited Indian chieftains to a feast and inadvertently fed them milk. The Indians, the experts theorize, who probably suffered from lactose intolerance, suspected they'd been deliberately poisoned and drove the Vikings off.

And if that isn't a perfect premise for a new TV series called *CSI: Newfoundland*, my name's Horatio Caine.

ARE YOU READY
FOR THE MENAISSANCE?

Okay. Listen up, all you hunky, hulking guys out there. I've got good news and I've got bad news.

The good news is: metrosexualism is dead. To which I can only add: amen, thanks be to Allah, and could you use an extra pallbearer for that coffin?

Metrosexualism—like disco and those tiny, shiny push scooters—was a fad that bloomed and disappeared before I had a chance to even think about signing on.

Just as well. I'm really not equipped.

You're familiar with metrosexualism, yes? It describes men who spend inordinate amounts of time (and money) preening and primping their image and lifestyle. You don't have to be gay to be a metrosexual, nor do you have to be straight. Fact is, sexuality is kind of immaterial to metrosexuals. They're in love with themselves rather than any particular gender. David Beckham is the poster boy for metrosexuals. Prince would make the cut, as would Tom Wolfe, Beau Brummell and Niles Crane of *Frasier*.

I don't think metrosexualism was mankind's finest hour and I'm delighted that it's defunct.

Now for the bad news: it's been replaced. By studliness.

And I mean *serious* studliness. Testosterone-drenched, beetle-browed, lineback-shouldered, monosyllabic caveman-type studliness.

And it all started with James Bond.

For years the chore of playing 007 fell improbably on the slim and sylphlike shoulders of Pierce Brosnan. Does he look like a guy who could snap a goon's neck with one hand while sipping a martini (shaken, not stirred) with the other? He does not. Pierce Brosnan looks like a guy who might audit for H&R Block or run a Vancouver hair salon.

Daniel Craig, on the other hand . . .

Craig is the new James Bond, and he's as far away from Pierce Brosnan as two body types can get. The Craig Bond is no elegant, effete-looking male-model type. He's muscular and knobby with a working guy's mug under a no-nonsense short-back-and-sides haircut. The distance between Brosnan/Bond and Craig/Bond was established memorably in the movie *Casino Royale* a couple of years ago. When a bartender asks Craig/Bond whether he prefers his martini shaken or stirred, he deadpans the guy and growls, "Do I look like I give a damn?"

If you really want to see what's hot and happening in the male image department, turn on your TV and watch an episode of *Holmes on Homes*. It's the TV home improvement program that stars Mike Holmes, a beefy, brush-cut fireplug of a man who dresses in bib overalls with a Stanley Kowalski undershirt peeking out from behind the bib. He's got a tattoo on one bulging bicep, and the leather tool belt slung around his waist is festooned with screwdrivers, pliers, hammers, a tape measure and other tools of the hard-nosed handyman's trade. When he's not actually ripping out shoddily constructed ceilings, floors, staircases and other assorted house features barehanded, Mike's fond of scowling darkly into the TV camera, his ham-hock arms folded across his barrel chest.

Mike Holmes does not look like the kind of guy whose Harley you'd want to cut off.

Mike Holmes looks like the kind of guy who could take Beckham, Brummell and Brosnan and karate-chop them into neatly stacked kindling.

Which is fine, I guess. It's nice to see old-fashioned masculinity rearing its low-browed head once more, but . . . must the pendulum swing so far? Good riddance to the poltroons and popinjays that personified metrosexualism, but must we regress all the way back to Neanderthal?

There's a guy by the name of Ethan Marak who maintains a blog on the web dedicated to manly matters. This is a recent excerpt:

> "It is time for . . . the reemergence of the beer-drinking, chick-shagging male stereotype—an old-fashioned man's man. It's time to run into the streets, belting out the Burger King manthem, 'I am man, hear me roar,' while chowing down on that Texas Double Whopper."

Oh dear.

Sounds a little too much like closing time at Moe's Tavern to me.

Suddenly Pierce Brosnan is looking good.

SAYONARA, SARNIA—
IT'S BEEN GOOD TO KNOW YA

I thought I might tell you a good news story.

Which is based on a bad news story. Remember my Sarnia adventure? Perhaps not. A recap, then.

Last November, straggling through the tail end of a book tour through southern Ontario, I became in seconds a man without a country.

Without an ID even. I had been flying from Toronto to Sarnia, Ontario. Somewhere in the 250-odd kilometres between those metropoli I dropped my driver's licence, never to see it again. It was the photo ID I had been using to board aircraft from one end of the country to the other.

As a matter of fact it was the only photo ID I was carrying. I had credit cards, a Canadian Legion card, a Canadian Tire card, an Aeroplan card—I had thirteen other pieces of identification that clearly indicated I was not an Al Qaeda, Taliban or Shining Path suicide guerrilla, but rather a pale, mild-mannered, geezer-type scribbler from west of the Rockies. The hawk-eyed minions of Air Canada would have none of it.

They wouldn't let me on the plane. Finally, after six hours of frenetic faxing of documents—my passport, birth certificate, social insurance card—by my long-suffering spouse on the far side of the country, the defenders of Sarnia sovereignty relented and let me pass.

Understand that I had no weapons. I had scrupulously jettisoned a lethal-looking pair of toenail clippers before I even got to the airport. I displayed my toothpaste and shaving cream in the Homeland-Security-mandated clear plastic bag for all to see.

Understand, too, that I was not in transit from the Excited States of America, where a Canuck expects to be treated like a bomb-toting Bolshevik. I was in rural Ontario, for God's sake, where the closest thing to a military target was a Tim Hortons or a Home Hardware with some leftover Halloween firecrackers.

Did I get mad? Hell no. I got even. One of my favourite writers, Nora Ephron, has a sign over her computer. It reads, "Everything is copy."

It's true. One of the great things about being a newspaper columnist is that no matter what happens, I can usually turn it into a 750-word Op Ed piece that runs in the paper the next day. I wrote a column about the idiocies of our airport security paranoia.

The next day I saw an email in my Inbox tagged "from the mayor of Sarnia."

Oops. Before I opened it, I Googled "mayor Sarnia" and learned that a guy named Mike Bradley had held that post for the past sixteen years.

He was either very good at his job or he was playing by the Fidel Castro rulebook.

Open the email? Or phone my lawyer? I opened the email. Here's what it said.

Dear Mr. Black:

Just read your column about your book tour that brought you to Sarnia, Ontario and your encounter with Air Canada's security. While you may mock us, the safety and security of our 993 Tim Hortons is of paramount concern for the citizens of this City and the Airport is a prime entry point. Thus our airport security is second to none.

Did you meet Bob our security guard? He doesn't have a gun but does have a whistle and is trained to use it on anyone who gets in the wrong line. What did you think of the 3 foot security fence? How about the X-ray machine borrowed from a local dentist? You may have been partially responsible for your own problems beyond the lack of photo ID. Were you in Air Canada's terrorist or non-terrorist line? They are very Canadian and if you were in the wrong line you would have been placed on double secret probation immediately by Bob. I apologize for the lack of a coffee machine, however; the machine was removed so no terrorist could hold a hot cup of coffee to a pilot's throat or even worse make him drink it and demand the plane be flown to Petrolia or Oil Springs instead of Toronto.

I have checked with Bob and he says it's not our fault locally because apparently anyone who works for the CBC is automatically put on the Terrorist Watch List by the Harper Government.

Cheers
Mayor Mike Bradley

Wow. Imagine having a mayor with a sense of humour like that. It's enough to make you want to vote for the guy. It's enough to make me want to go back to Sarnia even.

By train, mind you.

THE LONG AND
THE SHORT OF IT

*When I was a kid, I was so short I had to blow my
nose through my fly.*

—RODNEY DANGERFIELD

Quiz time, kiddies. Guess what the following five celebrities
have in common:

Avril Lavigne. Yuri Gagarin. Dudley Moore. Margaret
Mead. Prince.

The answer is: the tippy-tops of their heads are all precisely
157.48 centimetres from the soles of their feet. They are all, as
we used to say, five foot two inches tall.

(Okay, for Prince I stretched the truth. He's really five foot
two and a half.)

Why the focus on altitudinally challenged folk? Put it down
to an article I read in the paper recently. A judge in Lincoln,
Nebraska, decided to give Richard Thompson, convicted of
sexual assault, a sentence of ten years' probation instead of ten
years in jail.

Why? Because the judge figured Thompson, at five foot
one, was "too short" to survive in a state prison.

Many observers were outraged, but as secretary for the National Organization of Short Statured Adults, Joe Mangano was thrilled.

"I'm assuming a short inmate would have a much more difficult time than a large inmate," said Mr. Mangano (five foot four). "It's good to see somebody looking out for someone who is a short person."

I'm not convinced. It's my experience that short people can more than take care of themselves. Consider the relative elevation of some historical tough guys who would never have made anybody's basketball team: Soviet leader Nikita Khrushchev, five foot three. Marquis de Sade, five foot three. George "Baby Face" Nelson, five foot four. Horatio Nelson, five foot five. Joseph Stalin and Napoleon Bonaparte, five foot six.

Lack of height has never been an impediment for the saintly among us either. Gandhi was but five foot three. Saint Francis of Assisi was five foot one, and Mother Teresa scooted under the radar at four foot ten.

Artists? Gustav Mahler was only five foot four. Harry Houdini was barely five foot five, as is Pamela Anderson (we're talking vertically, remember). Michael J. Fox and Pablo Picasso: five foot four. Bo Derek and Judy Garland: five foot three. As for Gloria Swanson, Toulouse-Lautrec and Edith Piaf, none of them even broke the five-foot barrier.

And the English poet Alexander Pope has to be the patron saint of short creative people everywhere. The literary giant topped out at four foot six.

I have a soft spot in my heart for short people because I used to be one. I was born the runt of the litter and I remained a shrimp among sharks right through my adolescence. First guy to get towel-snapped in the locker room, last guy to get picked for the baseball team. The year I turned sixteen, I went to sea and put on thirteen kilograms of muscle and nearly thirty centimetres in height. I joined the ranks of the so-called normal, but I remember what it was like being a short guy.

Shortness can make or break you. It all comes down to attitude. There's a story about a woman who wakes up to discover that every hair on her head has dropped out but three.

"I think I'll wear a braid," she says.

The next morning, she wakes up to discover she has only two hairs on her head.

"I believe I'll part my hair right down the middle," she says.

The third morning, there is only one hair on her head.

"I'm going to try a ponytail," she says.

On the fourth day, she wakes up bald as a cue ball.

And says, "Oh, goody! I don't have to fuss with my hair!"

Shortness can be like that. There was once a British philosopher by the name of Dr. Richard Busby. He was five foot one. One day in a coffee shop he was accosted by a hulking Irish baronet who sneered, "May I pass to my seat, O giant?"

"Certainly, O pygmy," said Dr. Busby with a smile.

The Irish baronet tried to apologize. "My expression, ah, alluded to the size of your intellect," he stammered.

"And my expression to the size of yours," said the doctor.

I liked Fiorello La Guardia's style even better. Someone once asked the famous New York mayor how it felt to be the shortest man in the room.

La Guardia beamed and said, "Like a dime among pennies."

HE DOTH BESTRIDE THE WORLD LIKE A COLOSSUS

Try this on for size: *All's Well That Ends Well* by H. Neville. Nah.

How about *The Merchant Of Venice* by Hank Neville? Would you buy *King Lear* by Sir Henry Neville?

Nope—doesn't sing. It is, however, the latest half-baked premise in a series of unlikely theories and preposterous propositions, all seeking to discredit the legacy of William Shakespeare.

There is an entire lit-crit genre manned by a tireless subcategory of academic drones dedicated to the belief that the writer who gave us thirty-eight plays and uncountable sonnets and poems could not possibly have been the man history identifies as William Shakespeare.

How could—these Bard-knockers argue—a simple, homespun son of a failed wool merchant from hicksville Stratford-upon-Avon, how could this rube who never went beyond grammar school and couldn't even spell his own name the same way twice, how could such a bumpkin possibly write so knowledgeably and luminously about love and death and royalty and warfare and psychology and politics in places as far flung as Rome and Edinburgh, Elsinore and Athens?

No, they say. Clearly the author was someone infinitely more illustrious. Sir Francis Bacon perhaps. Or the poet Christopher Marlowe. Or the scholar-philosopher Edward de Vere.

Or, more lately, Sir Henry Neville.

Who he? An English courtier and distant relative of Shakespeare who, his champions reason, preferred to remain anonymous and let Shakespeare take the credit because he "wanted a poor relation to have a hand up."

Yeah, that sounds reasonable. Next year I'm going to pen a sequel to *War and Peace*, but I'll say my penniless niece in North Battleford wrote it.

Poor Shakespeare. All he did was bequeath the planet with the greatest literary legacy in the history of the English language. All his detractors want to do is erase his name on the title page.

Not fair. We owe him. And not just for the immortal comedies and tragedies, most of which the majority of us have never read and never will. Shakespeare didn't just transform English literature; he sprinkled the very tongue we speak with pixie dust. He touched us all at every level of communication, written and oral, and still does, each and every day. Consider this sentence:

"The sanctimonious and unearthly arch-villain bedazzled the vulnerable and fashionable go-between with honey-tongued and lustrous embraces and dauntless nimble-footed outbreaks of inauspicious pandering."

Every word in that (admittedly goofy) sentence—excepting "the," "and" and "of"—sprang from the brain of the bumpkin from Stratford-upon-Avon.

Despite the hyenas of academe nipping at his heels, Will Shakespeare of Stratford continues, almost four centuries after his death, to speak to—and for—all of us.

Will Sir Henry Neville even get a passing credit in the

Shakespeare sound-alike contest? Not likely. Jonathan Bate, author of *The Genius of Shakespeare*, says, "There's not a shred of evidence to support the [Neville-as-Shakespeare] argument; it's full of errors. There's no reason to doubt that Shakespeare wrote Shakespeare."

Ah, but why does he endure so? How does he continue to, as he once wrote of Julius Caesar, "bestride the world like a colossus?" Dominic Dromgoole, artistic director of the Globe Theatre said it best:

"He celebrated all the world, not just the section he favoured. We keep going back to him—now more than ever—because we know that his spirit of inclusion, his love of everything, is our last best hope."

THiS COUNTRY iS
GOiNG TO POT

When I was in my late teens, I lived for a time in a relatively seamy section of Montreal. My landlord, a wannabe jazz saxophonist, used to get together with an overgrown flower child who answered to the name Posey. They would spend most afternoons sitting on a balcony overlooking Rue Guy, puffing on doobies the size of panatelas as they giggled at the world going by.

They were the only two people I knew in the world who smoked pot.

Today—nearly half a century, legions of narc squads and several hundred million anti-drug dollars later—pot is being sold by kids to kids in schoolyards from Pangnirtung to PEI. I smell its sweet, sharp scent pretty much every time I walk past the park in the middle of town. So much for winning the war on drugs.

We've always been a little nutsoid about this backyard weed. The Americans can largely blame J. Edgar Hoover, the cross-dressing paranoiac who ran the FBI with an iron fist for most of the twentieth century. He's the guy who made sure Americans were taught that marijuana was as evil as heroin, serial axe murderers and devil worship.

We Canucks can thank Emily Murphy.

Ms. Murphy was a pioneer of women's rights in Canada. She became the first woman police magistrate in the British Empire back in 1916. She was instrumental in seeing that women were regarded as persons under Canadian law.

Then there was her other side.

She practised journalism and had a regular column in *Maclean's* magazine that she wrote under the pen name Janey Canuck. She used her column as a bully pulpit to pitch her personal war against drugs—specifically marijuana—and more specifically against the people who used it.

"Chinese, Assyrians, Negroes and Greeks," she assured her readers, were responsible for the presence of marijuana (she spelled it "marahuana") in Canada. She crusaded against letting such foreigners into the country. For those who were already here, she argued for compulsory sterilization—indeed, she wanted this for all "lesser humans" whom she complained were polluting the gene pool.

She worried in print that the white race was faltering, while the more prolific "black and yellow races may yet obtain the ascendancy" and thus threatened to "wrest the leadership of the world from the British."

When it came to the evils of pot, she really let her hair down. In her *Maclean's* column she wrote:

> Persons using this narcotic, smoke the dried leaves of the plant, which has the effect of driving them completely insane . . . Addicts to this drug, while under its influence, are immune to pain, and could be severely injured without having any realization of their condition . . .

They become raving maniacs and are liable to kill or indulge in any form of violence to other persons, using the most savage methods without any sense of moral responsibility.

The powers that be bought into Murphy's loopy argument. The laws of the country were revamped so that marijuana joined the ranks of heroin, cocaine and methamphetamines.

A weed that grows freely in ditches and barnyards became a criminal substance, possession of which could put you in jail.

And it stuck. In 1961, nearly thirty years after her death, any Canadian found with even a few grams of marijuana in pocket or purse could be sentenced to seven years in the slammer. Who knows how many thousands of Canadians have been arrested, charged, and in many cases thrown into jail as a direct result of Emily Murphy's delusional rantings?

Interestingly, marijuana is making a comeback. Not so much as a recreational drug (that's a constant) but as legitimate medicine. Many chronic pain sufferers swear cannabis is the only remedy that brings them relief. And a recent study published in the science journal *Molecular Pharmaceutics* claims that smoking marijuana may help stop the onset of Alzheimer's.

Alzheimer's is, of course, a disease characterized by memory loss, poor decision-making and loss of language skills.

Which is pretty much what happens to you when you smoke a joint.

Emily Murphy wouldn't appreciate the irony, but my old Montreal landlord would get a giggle out of it.

PHILIP THE LOOSE-LIPPED

I don't know exactly how the 2010 Olympics will go down in the history books, but I do know the organizers did one thing right.

They didn't invite Prince Philip.

This is a clever tactic, because Prince Philip has a tendency to verbally torpedo just about any project he's associated with.

In any case, Philip's already booked, Olympics-wise. He's scheduled to take part in the opening and closing ceremonies for the 2012 Olympics in London.

Good luck, London. Asked by newspaper reporters to describe his participation in the games, Philip harrumphed that he fully intends to do "as little as possible."

"I am truly fed up with the opening and closing ceremonies. They are a pain in the neck. Absolute bloody nuisances. I haven't been to one that wasn't absolutely, appallingly awful."

Tell us how you really feel, Phil.

Great Britain has already given us Richard the Lion-Hearted, Edward the Confessor and Ethelred the Unready. Make way for Philip the Loose-Lipped.

This is the diplomat who, addressing British students in Beijing, warned them "if you stay here much longer you'll all be slitty-eyed."

Philip is the smooth talker who asked a driving instructor in Scotland how he managed to "keep the natives off the booze long enough" to pass their driving test.

Canada has not escaped the back side of Philip's tongue. On being served yet another fish dinner during a royal visit to Nova Scotia in 1977, Philip moaned, "If I have to eat any more salmon I shall swim up a river and spawn."

On a royal visit to Calgary, he was presented with the requisite white ten-gallon Stetson. At which he bawled, "Oh God, not another one!" He later elaborated, "Once given the key to the city you don't go on getting keys to the city."

Philip is not only blunt, he has an undernourished attention span. In Vancouver in 1971 he was expected to officially bless a newly constructed annex to City Hall. Philip chafed visibly as politician after politician stood up and droned on about the architectural splendour, the cultural significance, the signal honour, blah, blah and blah. Finally, when it was his turn to officially pronounce the building up and running, Philip strode to the microphone and said, "I declare this thing open, whatever it is."

He later confessed that he had forgotten the name. "It was raining, and I wanted to get on with it: especially as the total audience was about fifteen passing shoppers under umbrellas." Apparently Vancouverites agree with Philip's underwhelmed reaction. To this day the annex is known as the East Thing.

Prince Philip is a curmudgeon's curmudgeon. He can get away with it because he's an octogenarian. But the truth is, he's always been crude by royal standards—and decidedly arrogant.

But you know what? I like it. The man is honest. A blue-blooded lager lout. Archie Bunker in ermine. Wouldn't you prefer to hear Philip's not-so-*bon mots* over the banal utterances of just about any politician of any stripe these days?

There's a book by Joe Klein called *Politics Lost: How American Democracy Was Trivialized by People Who Think You're Stupid.* Klein's theme is that political pronouncements have been dumbed down to the point where anything a politician says is so bland as to be meaningless. He's right. Think George Bush and his "Amurrica is about freedom" mantra. Do you remember any word or phrase uttered by Paul Martin when he was PM? Every time he opened his mouth he sounded like a duck caught in a leghold trap. Stephen Harper is no better. He sounds like Mr. Dressup, talking in a simple, rhythmic cadence like a dad reciting a fairytale to a sleepy child.

Which, come to think of it . . .

Nope, give me splenetic, old, politically incorrect, shoot-from-the-lip Phil—who to be fair, can be witty and self-deprecating. Once in Australia, he was introduced to a "Mr. and Dr. Robinson."

"My wife is a Doctor of Philosophy," explained Mr. Robinson. "She is much more important than I."

"Ah, yes," replied Prince Philip. "We have that problem in our family too."

But Philip doesn't always have the final word. On a visit to the city of Brasilia, he asked a Brazilian admiral about the colourful strip of medals on his chest.

"Did you earn those on Brasilia's artificial lake?" he sneered.

"Yes sir," replied the admiral with a disarming smile. "Not by marriage."

WELCOME TO EARTH.
HAVE A CHICKEN WING?

The world of advertising loves to give us human icons that are larger than life—some real, some fake. Mr. Clean is an obvious fiction—a cartoon, in fact. The Man from Glad is real—or as real as actors get. The Marlboro Man? He was an interesting mix. Or rather they were. Over the twenty-year course of the ad campaign, more than a dozen actors donned Stetsons and chaps and stuck a Marlboro in their grizzled mugs to portray the quintessentially macho Marlboro Man. They sure looked authentic. Two of the actors, David McLean and Wayne McLaren, even died of lung cancer.

That's carrying method acting a little too far.

Other advertising brands were totally bogus. There never was an Aunt Jemima or a Betty Crocker. As for that old poseur "Kentucky Colonel" Sanders—hah! Only a Madison Avenue copywriter could come up with a fat guy in a Mark Twain suit, string tie, horn-rimmed glasses and a snow white goatee intoning "Mmmm! Finger-lickin' good!"

Well, actually, the Colonel wasn't a fraud. He really lived and he really did fry and serve up chickens based on, as the ads said, his own recipe of "11 secret herbs and spices."

Harlan David Sanders was born in Henryville, Indiana, in 1890. After several abortive early careers as a fireman, steamboat skipper and insurance salesman, he ended up, at age forty, running a gas station in Kentucky and serving chicken dishes on the side.

Before too long the gas pumps were growing cobwebs and Sanders was running out of dinner plates. He quit the service station business, bought a restaurant and made himself the chef. His chicken dinners became so famous the governor of Kentucky dubbed Sanders an honorary Colonel. Sanders treated it like a knighthood and started dressing like a typical old-time Kentucky gentleman. His chicken franchises took off, and Colonel Sanders became the second most famous face of the South, right after Elvis.

In 1964, when the Colonel was pushing seventy-five, he put down the frying pan, sold the KFC name and accepted a position as roving ambassador for the company.

An ambassador, but not a mouthpiece. When he felt the quality of food was going down, he called a press conference and said so. He called the gravy being served "sludge" and said the mashed potatoes tasted like "wallpaper paste."

Sanders was so outspoken that the Kentucky Fried Chicken people actually sued him for libel. They lost, and for the rest of his life the Colonel continued to fire verbal broadsides whenever he thought the business was sullying the brand name he founded.

Sanders died in 1980—which is to say his corporeal form disappeared from earth—but the Colonel lives on, thanks to some fourteen thousand KFC restaurants around the world, seventeen hundred of which are in China. If Canadians get a yen for a bucket of grease, they have 786 KFC outlets to choose from. You'd think that would be enough market penetration to satisfy the folks at KFC, but you'd be wrong.

They're looking at Mars.

Today a UFO pilot cruising high over planet Earth would be able to make out the continents, the oceans, the Rockies, maybe the Great Wall of China . . .

And passing over Nevada—Great Klingon!—isn't that . . . the Colonel?

It is. In the middle of the Nevada desert, a one-hectare-sized image of Colonel Sanders—wearing a red-and-white striped apron in place of his trademark double-breasted suit—smiling up at the heavens. It is the world's first brand visible from space.

Reasonable people, after shaking their heads, might want to know, well . . . why?

Gregg Dedrick, president of KFC, explained with a straight face, "If there are extraterrestrials in space, KFC wants to become their restaurant of choice."

Heh, heh.

Reminds me of the story of another megalomaniacal earthling, Joseph Pulitzer. He was an early twentieth-century American press baron and owner of the *New York World*, a newspaper that, as he told anyone who would listen, deserved to be "more powerful than the president."

To that end he called a gaggle of flunkies into his office and ordered them to construct the biggest billboard in the world to advertise his paper. "I want it so big," growled Pulitzer, "that it could be read from Mars."

One assistant finally got up the courage to say, "Ah, fine, sir. And what language shall we print it in?"

DO YOU SPEAK STRINE?

E very Saturday morning I ease out of bed at five a.m., gently close the bedroom door and tiptoe down to the kitchen to hunch over the countertop radio. With my eyes on the kitchen clock and the volume turned down to a whisper, I listen to the last of the CBC newscast. The announcer signs off. There's a little sting of music and then . . . the words I've been waiting to hear.

"G'dye. Moi nyme iz Mick O'Regan and thiz . . . iz *The Sboats Vectuh*."

It's a program about sporting news from Down Under. In English it would be called *The Sports Factor*, but it's coming from the Australian Broadcasting Corporation and Mick is an Aussie jock, so it comes out "Sboats Vectuh."

The English language has undergone some merry and marvellous mutations as it percolated across the planet over the past few centuries. It's put forth blooms as various as Louisiana lilt and Highland burr, Hindu singsong and Ottawa Valley twang— but there is no English variant quite so ear-clangingly "stroiking" as the Australian dialect.

Or Orstrylian, to pronounce it properly.

Most people just call it Strine, and if you ever find yourself between two Ozlanders with a two-four of Foster's chatting in their mother tongue, you may doubt that what you're hearing has any connection to English whatsoever.

Australians have been pummelling the Queen's English ever since those first shiploads of deported British criminals got frog-marched ashore in Botany Bay back in the 1700s. There's still a strong hint of Dickensian Cockney in the language that comes out of an Australian's gob. As for when it became known as Strine, that's tough to pin down, but it might have been one afternoon in a bookstore in Sydney back in 1964 when British author Monica Dickens—a great-granddaughter, coincidentally enough, of Charles Dickens—was signing copies of her latest book for her fans. A dour-looking lady approached Ms. Dickens with a copy of the book in hand. "Would you like me to autograph that for you, Miss . . . ?" inquired the author pleasantly.

"Emma Chissett," the fan replied.

Odd name, thought Ms. Dickens, but she took the book, opened it to the flyleaf and wrote "To Emma Chissett, with sincere best wishes," then signed it with a flourish. She handed the book back to the woman. She wouldn't take it. "Emma Chissett," she said again.

Which was when the ha'penny dropped for Monica Dickens. The woman wasn't saying her name. She was asking, "How much is it?"—in Strine.

It can be very confusing. If somebody came up to you and announced, "Chair congeal et baked necks," you might be tempted to send for the white-coated gents carrying butterfly nets.

Relax. It's just a Striner telling you that "Jack and Jill ate bacon and eggs."

Once your ear becomes attuned, you will certainly hear semantic constructions you'd never hear anywhere else. When searching for an expression of mild disbelief, a Canadian might say "Imagine that!" or "My goodness!" A Strine speaker will exclaim "Starve the lizards!" or "Stone the crows!" A Striner would never be content with merely stating that something was in short supply. He would dub it "as rare as rocking horse poop."

Some Strine expressions make eminent, if colourful, sense. What's Strine for throwing up?

A Technicolor yawn.

How do you say someone is kind of . . . lame?

"As useless as a chocolate teapot."

Then there are the expressions that only make sense if you were born in the land of kangaroos, koalas and duck-billed platypuses. Try to take advantage of an Australian and you're liable to find yourself being lifted off the ground by a fist at your throat and a nasty voice growling, "Don't come the raw prawn with me, bucko!"

Don't come the raw prawn? What the hell could that possibly mean? Beats me, but once he sets you back down you could lay a classic Aussie curse on him: "I hope your chooks turn into emus and kick your dunny down!"

Don't ask me what that means either. Ask Emma Chissett.

FAR SIDE, WHERE ARE YOU?

He haunts us still.

Larson, I'm talking about. Gary Larson. The most hilarious cartoonist ever to pick up a Sharpie and skewer the world around him. It's been many long, deeply unfunny years since his quirky, warped, one-panel cartoons appeared in your newspaper and mine. At its peak, *The Far Side* was translated into seventeen languages and appeared in newspapers from Seattle to Singapore and from Montreal to Manchester.

Far Side cartoons were like no newspaper cartoons before or since. They were not only off the wall, they were out the door, down the street and out in the ozone.

Two polar bears hunched over an igloo, the top smashed in. One bear says, "Oh, hey! I just love these things! Crunchy on the outside and a soft, chewy centre!"

A family of squid driving in a sedan. A talking, cross-dressing snake who answers to Frank. A gaggle of grizzlies huddled around one of their confrères who sports a series of concentric circles like a bull's eye on his chest.

"Bummer of a birthmark, Hal," another grizzly mutters.

Gary Larson didn't hail from an artistic background. Back in the late sixties he was a biology major at Washington State University. One day it dawned on him that he had no idea what he would do with a biology degree, so he switched to communications, found that equally unfruitful, and wound up working as a clerk in a music store and spending his summers strumming banjo in a going-nowhere garage band duo called Tom and Gary. In 1976 he realized he basically hated the so-called professional side of his life.

Unaccountably and apropos of nothing, he drew a series of six single-pane cartoons featuring weird animals and geeky guys in lab coats. He submitted them to a local science magazine that bought them on the spot. On the strength of the double-digit cheque he received, Larson quit his day job and started drawing cartoons full-time.

His timing couldn't have been better. Our newspapers were full of vapid, insipid cartoon strips like *Mary Worth, Hi and Lois*, and that most execrable of newspaper staples, *The Family Circus*. Into this world of vacuity and brain death came *The Far Side* with cartoons about talking cows, licentious apes . . . and a caveman conducting a PowerPoint seminar for his colleagues. The screen shows a close-up of the spiked tail of a *Stegosaurus* dinosaur. The presenter, dressed only in a leopard skin, points to the tail and says, "Now, this end is called the Thagomizer . . . after the late Thag Simmons."

Oh hell. It's impossible to convey the intrinsic goofiness and breath-catching delight of a *Far Side* cartoon in words. You have to see them in all their black and white, one-panel glory.

And alas, we can't. Larson hit his peak in the mid-nineties with nearly two thousand newspapers carrying his strip around the world.

So what does a world-famous, impossibly successful cartoonist do when he's got the world by the gonads?

If he's Gary Larson, he quits, of course. In 1995, at the height of his fame, Larson announced that he was done.

Not for a couple of months. Not for a sabbatical. Not for a rest, to recharge the batteries.

For good.

He was only forty-four, but he could sense impending burn-out. "I didn't want to wind up in the Graveyard of Mediocre Cartoons," he told a reporter.

So what's Larson up to now? Mostly travelling the world with his sweetie (an anthropologist, fittingly enough) and studying jazz guitar. He hasn't left us completely *Far Side*-less. Every few years, it seems, another collection of old *Far Side* cartoons comes out. They keep us laughing—and remind us how hopelessly bland and toothless most other newspaper cartoons have become. When's the last time you laughed out loud at the moribund antics of *Dagwood*? Or *Dennis the Menace*? Or Canada's own once-brilliant, now soap-opera-mediocre *For Better or Worse*?

Far Side cartoons—even recycled ones—are infinitely better than that.

And even if the random collections stop coming out, Larson will be remembered—at least in the annals of science—for all time. He has been immortalized by the Committee on Evolutionary Biology at the University of Chicago. They've named a newly discovered species—the *Strigiphilus garylarsoni*—in his honour.

It's a biting louse found only on certain species of owls.

That's good enough to be a *Far Side* cartoon on its own.

THE BEST THINGS IN LIFE

EXERCISE: IT'S A DOG'S LIFE

The upright rowing machine did not work out. I had high hopes when I installed it in a corner of the bedroom two years ago. Here was the solution to my exercise problem, I told myself. Just a few minutes a day in the comfort of my home and I would at last earn those masculine accoutrements—rippling biceps, thighs like locomotive pistons and a rack of rock-hard abs you could smash walnuts on—that have eluded me since . . . well, forever, actually.

For two weeks I used the machine religiously every other day. But then something came up. A business trip perhaps, or maybe it was a writing deadline. In any case I fell out of the rhythm. One day I hung my warm-up jacket on the handlebars. It was still there four months later.

When fitness guilt descended again, I started pricing other kinds of exercise machines. But the major problem with machines is they're so . . . mechanical. No soul. Walking your buns off and getting nowhere on a treadmill is too much like real life. The Nautilus? I get stomach cramps just looking at it.

And sitting on a stationary bike spinning my wheels reminds me of that afternoon I spent stuck in a snowbank outside Sioux Lookout.

In the end I decided to go Hollywood and hire myself a personal trainer. Two, actually—a guy and a gal—just to ensure my physical prowess wasn't too gender-specific. Like all good personal trainers mine have a bit of a Nazi complex. They're incorruptible. "Finished your breakfast? *Gut!* Ve vill eggzerzize now." Not after you read the paper, finish your coffee or check your email. Now. And they let me know in no-nonsense, non-negotiable terms.

They bark.

My PTs are dogs—a bearded collie named Homer and a border collie and golden retriever cross who answers to Woolly. Their binding (though unwritten) contract guarantees them a forty-five-minute patrol of the neighbourhood commencing at 8:00 a.m. each and every morning, seven days a week, plus a late-afternoon romp in the local orchard complete with frisbees, tennis balls, Kongs-on-ropes and random sniffings of any other four-legged personal trainers that happen to show up.

Unlike most of my compromises with real life, using dogs to keep fit actually makes sense. Researchers at the University of Missouri, Columbia, studied the phenomenon and concluded that perambulating with your pooch provides the same benefits you receive when you hire a personal trainer—namely, it ensures you get off your duff and cardiovasculate even when your inner sloth is urging you to tackle nothing more challenging than the channel switcher.

How effective can regular dog walking be? According to an article in *Legion Magazine*—pretty darned. Rebecca Johnson, associate professor of nursing and director of the College of Veterinary Medicine's Research Center for Human-Animal Interaction, helped set up the study for the University of Missouri. "The results were wonderful," she says. "Our first study group averaged a weight loss of 14 pounds per person during the one-year program."

And these were not mush-you-huskies survival treks. The walkers started out with easy ten-minute walks three times a week. Eventually they worked themselves up to a leisurely twenty minutes five times a week.

Didn't change their diets, count calories or sign up at a spa. Lost an average of over six kilos each.

Don't own a dog—or want to? No problem—borrow someone else's. There are a lot of dogs out there not getting the regular exercise they crave. Ask the owner if you can take Rover for a walk. The owner—not to mention Rover—will love you for it.

But if you try it, sooner or later you'll probably want your very own in-house canine trainer. Downside? Walking a dog really is non-negotiable—neither rain nor sleet, etc. And while you're not lashing out dough for club dues, hundred-dollar training shoes and trendy Lycra exercise outfits, you will face veterinary bills, dog licence fees, training, grooming and sundry expenses for leashes, collars, toys, and of course, dog food.

It adds up. Churchill Insurance, a pet insurer in England issues an annual Cost of a Dog report. A recent one claims that the average cost of owning a dog (assuming a ten-year lifespan) runs to thirty-eight thousand dollars.

That'd buy a lot of Nordic Tracks.

But come on—when's the last time your Nordic Track licked your face?

THE SCOOTER: FOR A SHORT GUY HE CAST A LONG SHADOW

> *The one constant through all the years has been baseball. America has been erased like a blackboard, only to be rebuilt and then erased again. But baseball has marked time while America has rolled by like a procession of steamrollers.*
>
> —W.P. Kinsella, *Shoeless Joe*

I'm not much for baseball trivia. I couldn't name three guys in the Blue Jays lineup and I wouldn't know an ERA from an RBI from an NDP or an AFL-CIO.

But I know a baseball milestone when we reach it. That happened when Phil Rizzuto died.

It wasn't a big surprise. The guy was 89 and hadn't dressed for a game since 1954 when all television sets were black and white and Louis St. Laurent was our PM.

Even when he played shortstop, Rizzuto wasn't the flashiest guy on the field. He was a small man playing on a team that included legendary giants like Joe DiMaggio, Mickey Mantle and Yogi Berra. It's difficult to cast much of a shadow in company like that, especially when you only stand five-foot-six in your cleats and weigh less than the bat boy. And Rizzuto was no powerhouse slugger. Barry Bonds is flirting with eight hundred career home runs—Rizzuto hit only thirty-eight in his entire thirteen-year career.

"My stats don't shout," Rizzuto once remarked. "They kind of whisper."

Rizzuto won't be remembered so much for what he accomplished on the field. It was what he did in the broadcast booth that makes him a baseball immortal. The Scooter spent less than a decade and a half playing ball, but he spent the next four decades talking about it as the official announcer for all New York Yankees games.

And as an announcer, he broke every rule in the book. He was an unabashed homer. He loved the Yankees like family and barely acknowledged the teams they were playing. His favourite expression was "holy cow." He used it to described a Yankee double play, the sunset or the hot dog he had eaten at lunch.

He used air time to congratulate any of his friends who were celebrating a birthday or an anniversary. He would interrupt the play-by-play to send out best wishes to a pal laid up in hospital with a broken leg. He would keep Yankee fans *au courant* with news of his wife's shopping sprees and who came over for dinner last night.

He was also a flaming neurotic and he talked about that too. He told the fans how much he feared snakes. And rats. And lightning.

Also traffic. Rizzuto had an obsessive fixation about getting stuck in traffic. So much so that he once left the broadcast booth during the seventh inning in order to beat the other cars out of Yankee Stadium and get over the bridge to his home in New Jersey.

Hey. The Yankees had a big lead anyway.

Rizzuto was an oddball, but he was following a baseball

tradition of oddball commentators. Babe Ruth was once presented to King George VI during a North American royal tour. "Your majesty, may I present Mr. George Herman Ruth," intoned the master of ceremonies. "Mr. Ruth, this is King George VI."

"How ya doin', King?" said Ruth.

But it was Yogi Berra, a teammate of Rizzuto's who really gave The Scooter a run in the non-sequitur department.

The Yankee catcher's observations were frequently Zen-like. Watching Mickey Mantle and Roger Maris clobber back-to-back home runs, Berra murmured, "It's déjà vu all over again." He also said, "You've got to be careful if you don't know where you're going because you might not get there."

Most of the time Yogi's comments were just dopey. When asked if he wanted his pizza cut into four or eight slices, Berra said, "Better make it four . . . I don't think I could eat eight." His math wasn't so hot when it came to baseball either. "Ninety percent of this game," Berra said, "is half mental."

But little Phil Rizzuto holds the world record for most inappropriate comment on the air. During a ball game in 1978, the play-by-play was interrupted by a news bulletin that Pope Paul VI had died. After the bulletin, a chastened Rizzuto came back on the air with "Holy cow. That kind of puts a damper on even a Yankee win."

US baseball commissioner A. Bartlett Giamatti once wrote, "Baseball breaks your heart. It is designed to break your heart."

Well maybe. But it provides a lot of belly laughs along the way.

BLOWIN' IN THE WIND

*The tragedy of being famous is that you must
devote so much time to being famous.*

—Picasso

I see that Bob Dylan played a gig at Casino Rama.

Oh dear.

I know Casino Rama. It is a glitzy First Nations gambling complex that sits, improbably, in cottage country a couple of hours north and west of Toronto. It features a 300-room hotel, nine restaurants, over a hundred gaming tables and 2,400 slot machines. At the front entrance you can watch a never-ending chain of Casino Rama buses disgorging retirees, pensioners and way too many young and gullible hopefuls from towns and cities all over southern Ontario. They come to play blackjack, roulette, Texas Hold'em and of course the one-armed bandits. The bus rides are free. Casino Rama knows it's going to get its money back. I was in Casino Rama once, coming back from a gig of my own, hurrying to catch an early morning flight at Pearson International Airport. Driving down this winding secondary road in the pre-dawn murk I suddenly came upon what looked like an entire electrified city shimmering smack in the middle of nowhere. The parking lot was jammed. It was 5:30 in the morning.

I went in. It was bedlam. Lights flashed and strobed; bells gonged and clanged; horns hooted and buzzers buzzed. And all around me, row upon row of leaden-eyed zombies in ball caps and Bermuda shorts, hair curlers and Capri pants, sat glumly, stolidly feeding steady streams of loonies and toonies into slot machines.

It was one of the most depressing scenes I've ever witnessed.

But greed is a powerful urge, and so is the belief that you can get something for nothing. Are you a devotee of casinos? Then I'm sorry, but you are an idiot. I know why the gullible hordes show up. Sheep be always with us. The question is: what was Dylan doing there?

Dylan—love him or loathe him—is a rock 'n' roll giant. More musically talented than the Rolling Stones, more prolific than the Beatles. Granted, his voice is an adenoidal disaster, but his song-writing ability and his mastery of guitar and piano are second to none. He is a worthy peer of Elvis and Ella, Mama Cass and Johnny Cash.

Except Dylan is still alive.

And still on stage. He's on what he calls the Never Ending Tour and he's not kidding. In one recent month he played twenty-one concerts, ranging from Quebec and Ontario to Michigan and Ohio. The next month he did California, New Zealand, Australia, Texas and Illinois. He's been touring the world—month in, month out—for the past twenty-plus years.

He doesn't need the money. Dylan was a multi-millionaire when Kennedy was president. He doesn't need the fame. He's already achieved that level where a single name defines him. Like Garbo, Elvis, Diana, OJ.

He doesn't need to play a fifty-buck-a-night whistle stop like Casino Rama. He can sell out the Royal Albert Hall and the Hollywood Bowl, not to mention Massey Hall or the Air Canada

Centre. So why the Hicksville gigs in Illinois and Wisconsin? Why Casino Rama in rural Ontario?

Colleen Sheehy, director of education of Weisman Art Museum in Dylan's home stomping grounds of Minnesota, says, "I think he's always doing unexpected things that throw people off trying to pin him down, so it doesn't surprise me that, at this peak in his career, he would choose a down-and-out place to play. I think he identifies with down-and-out places, and with peoples' lives that might not be going anywhere."

That would all too accurately describe the killing floor of Casino Rama all right. But I think perhaps Charles Lindbergh got it best. The man who flew the first solo non-stop flight across the Atlantic knew a thing or two about the withering force field of fame. "At first you can stand the spotlight in your eyes," he said. "Then it blinds you. Others can see you, but you cannot see them."

I think of Dylan, pushing seventy, with nothing left to prove, jumping up on yet another stage on yet another evening some-where in the world, the lights blazing down on him, the crowd cheering yet again.

I think of something he said in one of the hundreds and hundreds of songs he's written:

> I've been walking through the middle of nowhere
> Trying to get to heaven before they close the door.

Vaya con Dios, Mr. D.

ART, FOR PETE'S SAKE

If the artist has total freedom—if art can be anything the artist says it is—it will also never be anything more than that.

—PETER FULLER

Take a stroll with me along Crosby Beach, just north of Liverpool, England. Do you see that naked man, up to his ankles in the incoming tide, staring out to sea?

Get used to it. There are ninety-nine more just like him along this three-kilometre stretch of shingle and they are all doing the same thing.

They are statues, life-sized, in cast-iron. Together they make up an art installation called *Another Place*. They are the work of British sculptor Antony Gormley, and most people—myself included—think they are a Beautiful Thing. Initially there was some grousing from environmentalists, sea anglers and windsurfers, but most people have fallen in love with the statues. "They are awe-inspiring," says one visitor. "I had to go and touch them . . . I'd really like to spend a long time with them. I can sense their hesitation, that feeling of 'Shall I, shall I not, go in.'"

On the other hand, come with me to the famous Tate Gallery in London. There we will see an exhibit called *Bed*. It consists of a mound of precisely 8,640 slices of Mother's Pride white bread that have been arranged to resemble a typical double mattress.

From which the artist has fastidiously eaten away an imprint equal to the shape and volume of his own body.

Well, not eaten, exactly. The artist chewed the bread into desired shapes, then dipped the gobs of bread in paraffin to prevent mould and dried the bread on radiators in his house.

The demented detritus of a committable fruitcake? Don't be too hasty. The sculptor of *Bed* is Antony Gormley, the same guy who did *Another Place*.

But it's easy to understand how one might get confused. The art world is a bewildering place these days. Even the experts have trouble sometimes. Another British sculptor, David Hensel of Sussex, recently submitted a piece to the Royal Academy of Art. It was a simple display consisting of a bone and a rock. They really liked it. One judge particularly mentioned its "minimalist intensity."

But it turned out the curator hadn't completely unpacked Hensel's submission. The bronze head that he'd submitted was still in the crate. The work of art they'd lauded was in fact the support for displaying the bronze.

Or take the trial in Dresden, Germany, where Petra Kujau, a somewhat dodgy art dealer, was recently charged with selling some five hundred fake paintings, supposedly signed by artists from Monet to Van Gogh to Picasso.

Well, big deal. Selling fake paintings is a crime, right? She deserves to go to jail.

It's not that simple. The buyers knew the paintings were forgeries. Frau Kujau's crime was trying to pass them off as fakes painted by her great-uncle, one of the master forgers of all time. So she is guilty of misrepresenting run-of-the-mill fakes as . . . classic fakes.

Not confused enough yet? Come with me to the Chapter Arts Centre in Cardiff, Wales. If we hurry we can catch Simon Pope's show. It's called Gallery Space Recall.

It's an empty room.

Well, not entirely empty. There is a printed list of instructions directing visitors to close their eyes and imagine another art show that they've seen recently, so that the exhibits "can exist at two locations simultaneously, both here and there." Pope said he got his inspiration for the exhibit by reading a medical textbook on brain-injury disorders. Apparently there is a condition known as "reduplicative paramnesia" in which the afflicted person has the delusional belief that something exists at two places at once.

No wonder some of us have trouble keeping up with the art world.

Like the two art lovers swooning over a canvas at the Metropolitan Museum of Art. "I wonder who the artist was," mused one. Her friend leaned in to read the bronze plaque next to the painting.

"It says it was painted by Circa, in 1878," she reported.

"Oh," said the first art lover, "Of course! Circa the Greek!"

"No," said her companion. "You're thinking of Zorba. Circa was Italian."

IN DOG WE TRUST

> *If you pick up a starving dog and make him*
> *prosperous, he will not bite you. This is the*
> *principal difference between a dog and a man.*
> —MARK TWAIN

> *You can say any foolish thing to a dog, and the dog*
> *will give you this look that says, "My God, you're*
> *right! I would never have thought of that!"*
> —DAVE BARRY

The wedding, which took place in a small village in India, was traditional—sort of. The groom—one P. Slevakumar—strictly observed each precise procedure in the sacred Hindu ceremony. The bride, splendidly turned out in a gorgeous matrimonial sari, sat through the rites wordlessly, gazing up adoringly at her husband-to-be. It was a scene that had played out for hundreds of years and for hundreds of thousands of Indian brides before her.

Well, there was one small difference. This bride was a real bitch. I mean that she had four legs. And a tail. P. Slevakumar was marrying a dog.

It was an atonement thing. Fifteen years earlier, on the outskirts of the village, the man had callously stoned two dogs to death. Bad karma.

"After that my legs and hands got paralyzed," he explained. "I also lost hearing in one ear."

In desperation, Mr. Slevakumar consulted an astrologist who told him he could make amends by finding an amenable canine companion and making an honest . . . er . . . dog of her.

No word so far on how that marriage is working out, but it got me to thinking. Isn't that typical? Of a dog, I mean? Did anyone stop to ask the bride if she had any feelings about the marriage? Of course not. Dogs do what they're told. They are the original Uncle Toms of the pet world.

Try getting your cat to fetch a tennis ball. She will give you an incredulous look, as if to say, "Who? Moi?" And then resume washing her paws.

Whereas Fido will chase that ball down and bring it back until your throwing arm or his heart gives out.

T'was ever thus. Dogs, God bless 'em, are the original practitioners of unconditional love. We use them, abuse them, feed them scraps from our table, leave them out in the rain—they still treat us like gods. Doesn't matter if you're a dot-com gazillionaire or a squeegee kid sleeping in a refrigerator carton, if you've got a dog he'll stand by you till the deal goes down. That's what dogs do.

Fame? Doesn't come their way often. Oh, they had a couple of TV series—*Lassie, Rin Tin Tin*—and a couple of movies—*Old Yeller, 101 Dalmatians*. But that's a pretty small return for the eons of uncritical devotion that dogs have lavished on us.

Mind you, a few dogs have enjoyed their moment on the political stage. Canada's thirteenth prime minister, John "Dief the Chief" Diefenbaker, got off a good one at a press conference back in the early sixties when his popularity across the country was plummeting. A reporter asked him if he'd seen the latest

Gallup Poll. The Chief—eyes blazing, wattles quivering—thundered, "Poles? Poles? You know what dogs do to poles!"

And then there was Pat. Actually there were three Pats, all Irish terriers, all belonging (successively) to Canada's tenth prime minister, the slightly loopy William Lyon Mackenzie King. Mr. King was eccentric in the extreme and often made it clear that Pat (be it One, Two or Three) was his closest confidante.

There is no evidence that the PM consulted with his Irish terriers over crucial government decisions—his shaving mirror and his dead mother, yes, but not his dogs.

I would be remiss if I didn't mention dogdom's low point in the world of politics. That would involve US President Richard Nixon and his sad-eyed spaniel, Checkers.

Back in 1952, when then vice-presidential candidate Nixon was facing charges of receiving payola from wealthy Californians, he commandeered the national air waves to deliver his famous Checkers speech. Nixon told viewers he was willing to return any gifts he "might have" received—except for a little black-and-white cocker spaniel, Checkers, which had been given to his daughters. A photo of Checkers, looking adorable, was then flashed on the screen. It was cheap. It was cynical. It was exploitive. It worked like a charm. And poor Checkers got to serve as a prop for a sleazy politico.

It shouldn't happen to a dog.

THE BEST THINGS IN LIFE ARE CHEAP

Mini-confession right off the top: I haven't seen my own face for about a quarter of a century.

Most of it, anyway. I am a beardo—I've worn chin fur since one morning way back in 1982, when I looked at my lathered-up mug in the bathroom mirror for the umpty-gazillionth time, realized that unless I took drastic action, I was condemned to repeat this dreary, potentially blood-letting ritual once a day for the rest of my natural . . .

So I took drastic action. Tossed my Gillette single-blade razor in the wastebasket.

I'd long ago given up on electric razors because—sorry Philishave, Ronson, Braun, Remington, Norelco et al.—electric razors do a lousy job. Lots of sound and fury signifying nothing much except a brutish buzz cut that has to be repeated in a few hours' time. What's the positive side of a nasty hand-held machine that's cumbersome and power-sucking, whines like a Ski-Doo and gives you razor burn?

Scraping hair off your face, manually or electrified—who needs it? I gave it up nearly three decades ago and let my face go au naturel.

Nor have I regretted it. Especially when I stroll down the aisles of my local Pharmasave and see what my jettisoned Gillette single-blade razor has morphed into.

Gillette's latest razor—oops, make that shaving system— boasts an injection cartridge that features six, count 'em, six separate blades, five in a row and a sixth on the back of the razor.

What's more, modern face scrapers are encouraged to invest in a Persian bordello's worth of salves, unguents and emollients designed to moisturize facial stubble into something like a field of ripe wheat ready for the combine. Then there's the actual shaving cream, of course. It comes in gooey mousses, aromatic gels, sleek tubes and powerful aerosol bombs in a variety of scents and tinctures, all of them expensive.

And it's all unmitigated BS, men. All you'll ever need for the closest, cleanest shave is a single sharp razor blade, a brush, a cake of ordinary soap and plenty of hot water.

End, as Tony Soprano would say, of story.

But we never seem to want it simple. We want it complicated and pricey. How else to explain the fact that consumers now line up for the privilege of buying drinking water—Evian, Perrier, Dasani—in tiny plastic bottles at prices that make what we shell out at the gas pumps look like a bargain?

We can get all the perfectly safe drinking water we want absolutely free out of the kitchen tap, but no thanks, I'd much rather fork over a couple of loonies for a half-litre of Gerolsteiner.

It doesn't make sense. But neither does the fact that Levi's is getting rich selling jeans with factory-made holes in the knees and rips up the butt. Used to be if you had a pair of pants that looked like they'd served as a doormat for a herd of stampeding longhorns, you either made them into glad rags or popped them in the thrift store drop-off box. Now they're marketed for top dollar as pre-stressed jeans. Go figure.

The ultimate consumer absurdity? I nominate The Idea Store, the latest branch of which just opened in Whitechapel, London, England.

"The Idea Store," carols a brochure, "is a drop-in centre where you can learn English, acquire job-seeking skills, get legal advice, study sign language . . . or chat with your friends or yak on your cellphone." There's a fee, of course.

Thanks anyway, but we've already got an Idea Store in my neighbourhood—minus the yakking and the cellphone chatter. What's more, there's no admission charge. It's absolutely free—and chock full of ideas.

We call it the public library.

EVERYTHiNG OLD iS NEW AGAiN

E nglish is a hungry language. That's why it goes out and pilfers other languages at will. Much of English was stolen directly from French and Latin. The rest is a mongrel mix of words and concepts snatched from tongues around the world. We pick-pocketed the Arabs for alcohol, macramé and safari. Caboose? We lifted that from the Dutch. Shampoo? A Hindi word. Winnipeg? Toronto? Ottawa? Those we ripped off the Indians in exchange for a lifetime supply of Bibles.

I even double-checked this in *Wikipedia*. Wiki? A Hawaiian word meaning "fast."

That said, there's a word we need to steal from the Germans: *schlimmbesserung*.

I know it's a mouthful, but we have no equivalent in English and we need one desperately. *Schlimmbesserungs* are multiplying like rabbits (from Middle Dutch *robbe*). A *schlimmbesserung* is basically a lousy improvement. Something fixed that wasn't broken. For most of us, a twenty-nine-speed, titanium-framed, microweight bicycle that disintegrates in the first pothole it hits is a *schlimmbesserung* compared to the indestructible CCM one-speed we used to be able to buy. Classic Coke was a *schlimmbesserung*, as are aluminum hockey sticks and those stupid, screaming, "sanitary" washroom hand dryers that leave you with a hearing impairment—and wet hands.

What I find heartening is the fact that we—some of us anyway—are turning up our noses at a few *schlimmbesserungs* and returning to The Good Old Ways.

Clotheslines are back. And so are scythes.

We used scythes to cut our grass for a thousand years until lawnmowers came along. Now that's beginning to look like a bad swap. According to an EPA report, every gas mower emits the same amount of emissions in one hour as forty new cars. Environment Canada says nearly three million of us mow our lawns every summer weekend. If we used scythes, the air would be cleaner, the noise level would improve dramatically and over a year Canadians would save forty million gallons of gas.

Plus we'd all be getting a pleasant upper body workout for free.

And clotheslines make such eminent sense it seems odd that they ever went away, but they've been banned in thousands of communities across North America. Homeowners' associations have decided that the sight of T-shirts, bedsheets, jeans and mum's dainties billowing in the breeze is a visual blight not to be tolerated. Some neighbourhoods actually mount clothesline patrols—station wagons manned by eagle-eyed busybodies cruising the streets on the lookout for backyard laundry infractions. Seems absurd that the supermarket sells packages of dryer sheets promising "fresh rain fragrance" when you can get the real thing for free outside.

South of the border, a lot of folks are waking up to the absurdity. Clothesline activists are mounting a national Right to Dry movement.

A while back in *La Belle Province* a group of protesters

launched a campaign to stop Hydro-Québec from damming the Rupert River. They argue that the province wouldn't have to drown an entire river ecosystem if people just altered their energy-gobbling ways. Fittingly the campaign featured ads printed on T-shirts and sheets hung on—you guessed it—a clothesline. This one was 120 metres long.

Clotheslines over automatic dryers? No contest, really. Dryers bang up your clothes, howl like banshees and suck up insane amounts of power. A clothesline gets you out in the fresh air and makes your clothes last longer and smell better.

When it comes to environmental awareness, the tide is slowly turning, but there are still some major reefs and shoals before us.

Like, for instance, Mary Peters.

Ms. Peters was the last US secretary of transportation and just one of the many talentless carpetbaggers and cronies appointed by the Bush administration on the basis of party loyalty rather than any demonstrated competence. When asked what was responsible for the collapse of that Minneapolis bridge that caused the death of thirteen motorists a while back, Ms. Peters didn't hesitate.

She blamed bicycles.

And pedestrians. And museumgoers and people worried about crumbling lighthouses. That's where too much of the transportation infrastructure money was going, she said, adding that projects like bike paths and cycling trails "are really not transportation."

Someone once said, "Stupidity is more difficult to control than evil." In Mary Peters, I fear, we may have encountered a double-barrelled threat.

Meanwhile I'm thinking of getting a bumper sticker for my bike. It will read: No Iraqis Died to Fuel This Vehicle.

IT WAS A DARK
AND STORMY NIGHT

*We were somewhere around Barstow on the edge
of the desert when the drugs began to take hold.
I remember saying something like, "I feel a bit
lightheaded; maybe you should drive . . ."and
suddenly there was a terrible roar all around us
and the sky was full of what looked like huge bats,
all swooping and screeching and diving around
the car, which was going about 100 miles an hour
with the top down to Las Vegas.*

Did I write that? I wish. Those are the first two sentences in
Hunter S. Thompson's classic *Fear and Loathing in Las Vegas*.
It's my all-time favourite literary opener.

Opening sentences are crucial for any writer. They're like
casting a dry fly into a school of largemouth bass. If the fly—or
the sentence—is attractive enough, you'll get a bite.

Hemingway was a master of the art of hooking readers.
Check the opening of *The Old Man and the Sea:* "He was an old
man who fished alone in a skiff in the Gulf Stream and he had
gone eighty-four days now without taking a fish."

Not a single unnecessary word. It would be pretty hard not to want to know the rest of that story.

Charles Dickens was no slouch at opening sentences, either, although more than a touch windier than Hemingway. This is how Dickens began his classic novel *A Tale of Two Cities:* "It was the best of times, it was the worst of times, it was the age of wisdom, it was the age of foolishness, it was the epoch of belief, it was the epoch of incredulity, it was the season of Light, it was the season of Darkness, it was the spring of hope, it was the winter of despair . . ."

That's not even the whole first sentence. Dickens chunters on for another sixty words before he throws in a full stop. Nevertheless, "It was the best of times, it was the worst of times" is one of the most-quoted openers in English literature.

And so is the opening of *Anna Karenina* by Leo Tolstoy: "All happy families are alike but an unhappy family is unhappy after its own fashion."

On the other hand, take a look at this opener:

> In my younger and more vulnerable years my father gave me some advice that I've been turning over in my mind ever since.
>
> "Whenever you feel like criticizing anyone," he told me, "just remember that all the people in this world haven't had the advantages that you've had."

To my mind, that's flat-out boring. The odds are very high that I would close the cover of any novel that began like that without reading another word.

My loss—those are the first few words of F. Scott Fitzgerald's *The Great Gatsby*, which some critics consider to be the greatest novel of the twentieth century.

Well maybe. But personally, I prefer almost anything written by the American writer Elmore Leonard. Here's how he starts his novel *Glitz:*

> The night Vincent was shot he saw it coming. The guy approached out of the streetlight on the corner of Meridian and Sixteenth, South Beach, and reached Vincent as he was walking from his car to his apartment building. It was early, a few minutes past nine.

Try putting that novel down without reading more.

For sheer rich imagery it's hard to beat Canada's own Rohinton Mistry. Here's the beginning of *A Fine Balance* describing a train journey in India:

> The morning express bloated with passengers slowed to a crawl, then lurched forward suddenly, as though to resume full speed. The train's brief deception jolted its riders. The bulge of humans hanging out the doorway distended perilously, like a soap bubble at its limit.

And if reading a fine writer like Mistry makes you despair of ever starting your own novel, take heart. There are openers and there are openers. A few years back, Wm. W. "Buddy" Ocheltree took the Bulwer-Lytton Fiction Contest prize for writing the worst conceivable opening line for a novel:

> She wasn't really my type, a hard-looking but untalented reporter from the local cat box liner, but the first second that the third-rate representative of the fourth estate cracked open a fifth of old Scotch, my sixth sense said seventh heaven was as close as an eighth note from Beethoven's Ninth Symphony, so, nervous as a tenth-grader drowning in eleventh-hour cramming for a physics exam, I swept her into my longing arms, and,

humming "The Twelfth of Never," I got lucky on Friday the thirteenth.

There now. Don't you feel better already?

WOT—STRİNE AGYNE?

I hadn't even sucked the froth from my first pint of Piper's Pale Ale when I caught, from the other side of the room, The Look.

Sitting at the bar. Big guy. Eyes like dum-dum bullets and staring right at me.

Not kindly either.

It's an occupational hazard when you write a column like this for a living. Every once in a while, something you write ticks somebody off. Every once in a while, someone who knows what you look like points you out to a guy you ticked off. And then you've got trouble.

He came across the room toward me like a great white shark swimming through groupers. Pulled up about five centimetres from my nose.

"Oi'm a bit dirty on you, myte," he growled. "Wuz thinking you moit need a kick up the Khybah!"

And then he smiled and relaxed. And so did I. He was just an Aussie responding to a column I'd written about Strine, the weird and wonderful language spoken and understood only by Down Unders—folks born and bred in Australia.

It's an amazing dialect, is Strine. The name is a corruption of "Australian," or "Orstryliun," as a practitioner would pronounce it.

What would you think if a stranger came up and told you that you had a gloria soam? He's merely admiring your digs—you have a "glorious home," is what he's saying.

How about if a stranger accosted you at the local pub and inquired, "Jegoda the footy?"

A correct response would be, "Nar. Dingo. Sartentv."

Let me translate. The stranger has asked, "Did you go to the football game?" And you have responded, "No, I didn't go. I saw it on TV."

You are quaffing a Foster's with an Oz expatriate in a Toronto bar, perhaps. You ask if your friend saw the game last night, where the Leafs blew out the Philadelphia Flyers, eight to zip.

"Eich nardly bleevit," murmurs the Ozzie.

He's saying, "I can hardly believe it."

He buys the next round. You thank him. He smiles and says, "Sleece tiger doo."

Strine for "It's the least I could do."

Aussie speech is not always so impenetrable. Australians are nothing if not plain-spoken. They say what they mean and they mean what they say. Is there any other country that would have a national campaign against drunk drivers featuring a poster that reads, "If You Drink and Drive Then You're a Bloody Idiot"?

When former Australian Prime Minister Bob Hawke was pestered by Japanese reporters to explain his mission to their country, he grabbed the microphone and said, "Look. I'm not here to play funny buggers."

Now in Australia that's a perfectly straightforward response. It simply means, "I am not here to mislead you or to split hairs."

Regrettably the Japanese translator was not terribly fluent in Strine. He rendered it as, "Look, I am not here to play laughing homosexuals."

It's not Strine's fault. Strine at its purest is clear and concise, blunt and forthright.

But like French wine, it does not always travel well.

When an Australian diplomat tried to explain to a French audience his delight at finally being assigned a position in the Australian Embassy in Paris, he turned philosophical, musing that, as he looked back on his diplomatic career, it appeared to be divided into two distinct portions: boredom before he came to Paris and excitement thereafter.

That's what he meant to convey. Unfortunately what came out was, "When I look at my backside, I find it divided into two parts."

SAY CHEESE!

Somebody—obviously a devoted cheeseophile—once described cheese as "milk's leap toward immortality." Personally I wouldn't leap too high in defence of cheese. There are lots of different kinds out there, and one man's cheddar is another man's gorgonzola.

Cheese and I didn't get off to a very good start. The rest of my family favoured—for unfathomable reasons—a gooey, fluorescent orange confection called Velveeta. They ate tubs of the stuff. As a kid I was a bottomless pit and a dedicated fridge raider. I would pluck out and hoover back just about anything that wasn't lashed to the refrigerator shelves—but never the Velveeta. I would have gnawed the rubber gasket off the refrigerator door before I'd sink to that level. To me Velveeta looked—and smelled—like a used diaper.

There's an irony there, because as I discovered in later life, a lot of delicious cheese, well . . . stinks. The cheese reek can range from a smell of unwashed feet to a nostril-searing, pass-the-bucket stench redolent of Junior's unwashed football uniform mouldering in a high school gym locker, with a hint of long-dead mouse thrown in.

It's a sadistic little game we play with our senses. We hoist a wedge of cheese to our face, and our nose cries, "Yuk!" But our taste buds croon, "Yum!"

Nine times out of ten the taste buds win. Gorgonzola reeks, but we eat it anyway. Roquefort and Munster cheeses are pretty whiffy. Camembert can make your eyes water, and there's a French cheese called Vieux Boulogne that paramedics should use to revive heart attack victims.

And Blue Stilton! Why, Blue Stilton smells so bad we . . .

. . . dab it behind our ears?

Thought you'd heard of everything? Figured that the weirdness quotient had been used up in a world where people pay for bottled water, voted for George Bush and accord celebrity status to airheads like Paris Hilton? Not quite.

Make room for Eau de Stilton.

It's a perfume being marketed by the Stilton Cheesemakers' Association, and yes friends, they are dead serious. A spokesman explained, while maintaining a straight face, "Our parfumier was able to capture the key essence of the [Blue Stilton] scent and recreate it in an unusual but highly wearable perfume."

Where do we go from here? Cheddar roll-on deodorants? Brie cologne? Parmesan face powder? I hate to see the Stilton gang getting into the perfume business. It can only lead to nasty rivalries as cheesemakers attempt to outskunk each other.

And that means sooner or later somebody's going to roll out the *casu marzu*.

Casu marzu is the plutonium bomb of cheeses. It is native to Sardinia, and fortunately seldom gets very far from its roots. *Casu marzu* doesn't travel well. In fact there's not an airline in the world that would let you bring it aboard.

It's kind of self-explanatory if you know Sardinian dialect. *Casu marzu* means "rotten cheese." Even if your nose is on strike, you can always tell if you've got some *casu marzu* on your plate.

It will be moving.

That's because *casu marzu* is riddled with dozens and dozens of living, wriggling maggots. They are fly larvae deliberately introduced in the fermentation process to give *casu marzu* its trademark runny, stinky character. Removal of the maggots prior to ingestion is optional. Purists like to crunch them along with the cheese.

If you ever do summon up the nerve to try some *casu marzu*, you might want to bring along a pair of safety goggles. The maggots are highly active and can jump up to fifteen centimetres when agitated.

And how does *casu marzu* taste? Awful, apparently. A food critic writing in the *Wall Street Journal* describes it as "a viscous, pungent goo that burns the tongue and can affect other parts of the body."

Indeed it can. Indulgers run the risk of intestinal lesions, nausea, vomiting, hallucinations and bloody diarrhea.

Cheese. I recently read a front-page story in a British newspaper that starts out, "A deranged cheese counter assistant has been convicted of terrorizing a leading Limehouse psychiatrist for more than a year."

Check the guy's passport. Sounds like a *casu marzu* junkie to me.

SMELL THE ROSES, LISTEN TO THE MUSIC

Here's a question for you. Suppose you were not the urbane, sophisticated and knowledgeable citizen we both know you to be. Suppose instead you grew up in a small, benighted outpost with no library, no newspaper and lousy TV reception. One day somebody plops a canvas in front of you. It's Leonardo da Vinci's famous painting the *Mona Lisa*. Here's my question. Would you know you were looking at a masterpiece, one of the greatest paintings of all time?

Or would you just see a picture of a country gal with bad hair and a slightly goofy smile?

How about poetry? Say you'd grown up never having heard of T.S. Eliot, Emily Dickinson or William Shakespeare. You're down at the Legion tucking into a cold one, and the guy on the next bar stool stands up and starts belting out a Shakespearian sonnet, "Shall I compare thee to a summer's day?"

Would you be enthralled? Or would you be trying to make urgent eye contact with the bartender?

I only ask because of something that happened on the subway platform at L'Enfant Plaza station in Washington, DC, recently.

It's 8 a.m. on a typical workday morning. Commuters are hustling on and off the trains on their way to work or maybe to Starbucks for a cuppa to go. Up against the wall there's a young guy, a busker in a baseball cap and blue jeans, sawing away on a fiddle. He's got an open violin case at his feet with a few coins in it.

He's playing energetically. He's being pretty much ignored by the streams of commuters eddying around him. Nobody smiles. Nobody looks up. Nobody applauds when he finishes one piece and begins another.

To be precise, 1,097 people will pass the fiddle player in the next forty-three minutes. A few—very few—will distractedly toss some small bills or spare change toward the violin case without making eye contact with the fiddler or even breaking stride.

Precisely seven (7) people will stop, interrupt their journey, change their plans—temporarily rearrange their priorities—to stay for a few moments and actually listen to the man play his fiddle.

Good ears. The busker playing the fiddle is Joshua Bell, who happens to be one of the finest violinists in the world. The music he's playing? Bach. Schubert. Beethoven. The fiddle he's playing it on? A Stradivarius. Worth US$3.5 million.

We know all the details of this subway vignette because it's a set-up. It was orchestrated by the editors of the *Washington Post*. Not only was the entire forty-three-minute performance video-taped, there's a star reporter by the name of Gene Weingarten standing by and taking notes.

It's an experiment to discover whether beauty depends on its context. We all know the *Mona Lisa* is a masterpiece because it's in the Louvre. We know Vivaldi is sublime because his music gets played in concert halls by world-famous virtuosi. But what happens if the *Mona Lisa* shows up in a garage sale? Who notices if Vivaldi gets played by a Bavarian Oompah band?

It's a variation on the old philosophical conundrum, "If a tree falls in a forest and no one is there to hear it, does it make a sound?" In this case it asks, "If an orchid blooms in a rat maze, does anybody smell the aroma?"

Not many. Just seven of the 1,097 commuters on the Washington subway that morning even paused to hear Joshua Bell.

Well, let me amend that. Seven *adults* paused. Reporter Gene Weingarten noticed one other curious thing. The cold shoulder that Bell got from the public was nothing if not democratic. He was ignored by whites and blacks, Hispanics and Asians, males and females, geezers, middle-aged folks and teenyboppers with iPods. But there was one demographic group that glommed onto Joshua Bell and his violin every time, without fail.

Children.

"Every single time a child walked past," wrote Weingarten, "he or she tried to stop and watch. And every single time, a parent scooted the kid away."

Moral of the story? The corny old cliché, I guess. Don't forget to stop and smell the roses.

Don't forget to enjoy the sunrise. Don't forget to listen to the music.

And never forget to learn from the kids.

CHEAP TALK? NOT VERY

You want some face time with Bill Clinton? I can make it happen, sweetheart.

Got a yen to break bread with Deepak Chopra? Arnie Palmer? Dr. Phil? Just say the word and it's a done deal, baby.

I can have you rubbing elbows with ex-astronaut Buzz Aldrin, ex-Prime Minister Maggie Thatcher, cycling monorchidist Lance Armstrong or Shaquille "The Real Deal" O'Neal—take your pick—in next to no time at all.

Actually you don't even need me to pimp your rendezvous. All you need is your chequebook.

All the aforementioned celebs are working denizens of the after-dinner speakers' circuit. Any one of them would be happy to come and give a speech at your annual pipefitters' convention, your monthly Rotarian coffee klatch—even your local book club.

For a price.

If you want to hear from Deepak or Buzz, it'll set you back somewhere between thirty thousand and fifty thousand

US dollars. A speech from Lance or Arnie will run you about seventy-five thousand US dollars for the evening.

Bill Clinton? Better cash in those beer empties. Slick Willie charges US$150,000 a pop.

Too pricey? Not to worry, there's a B-list. For around ten grand you can be entertained by Toronto Argonauts coach Michael "Pinball" Clemons—or ex-PM Joe Clark.

I play this game, too, albeit for less lucre. I deliver humorous talks to conventions and seminars, conferences and powwows—although my fee is so far below the aforementioned top guns it's laughable. Hint: you could have Donald Trump hector you for half an hour for two hundred thou, or for the same price, you could have me speak to your group once a day including weekends from Easter till the snow flies.

It's a sweet gig, all things considered. As an after-dinner speaker you get a free meal and you meet interesting people who drive you to and from the airport and put you up in a hotel.

You also get a cheque that hardly ever bounces.

Is it a decent way to make a living? Well, I have had approximately twenty-seven different kinds of jobs in my life, and I have to say that standing up on your hind legs to address a roomful of (usually) pleasant strangers is one of the easier assignments I've faced . . . ever tried tar and gravel roofing? Speechifying is not, however, a cakewalk. Most audiences are well-behaved, enthusiastic and interested in what you have to say.

And then there are The Others.

I remember my address to a convention of repo men a few years back. These are chaps who haul TVs from apartments and snatch car keys out of people's fists for a living. All evening my audience stared me down through squinty Dirty Harry eyes. No one cracked a smile for the duration of my entire speech. Applause was spotty and grudging. I think they were just waiting for me to finish so they could repossess the lectern.

And I'll never forget my evening with the Vancouver Bar

Association. It's not news that lawyers can be nasty creatures, but little did I know there was an inner cadre of legal weasels within the association who considered it a point of honour to drive the annual convention's guest speaker from the stage before he or she can finish a speech. They did it with catcalls, jeers, table thumping, foot stomping and bun tossing.

I knew I was in trouble when the guy who was introducing me got hit in the eye with a dinner roll.

But hostile audiences are the exception to the rule. Most often an encounter between an after-dinner speaker and his hosts is civilized, enlightening and entertaining for all concerned.

And once in a rare while, something magical happens. I remember speaking to an animal welfare group in Toronto a few years back. After my speech, which was well-received, the treasurer stood up to report on the group's financial situation.

It wasn't good. In fact it was so bad that I realized my speaker's fee represented a significant drain on its coffers.

Well, what the hell—I love animals. I stood up and blurted that I was waiving my fee. They could take that money and put it to good use.

Cheers all around. Everyone went home happy.

A few weeks later I ran into the treasurer and asked her what good use they had found for my money.

"Actually," she said, "we put it into a fund to get better speakers next year."

THE SEDUCTIVE SOUND OF SILENCE

*Man has turned his back on silence. Day after
day he invents machines and devices that increase
noise and distract humanity from the essence of
life, contemplation, meditation.*

—JEAN ARP

Ever had an MRI? Stands for magnetic resonance imaging.
It's basically a machine that scans your innards to see what's
out of whack—in my case a wonky hip. Think of it as an X-ray
on steroids.

It's a little freaky, getting an MRI. First they ask you to
remove all rings, necklaces, bracelets, anklets and metallic pierc-
ings, if any. Then they ask you if you have any bullets, arrow-
heads or other metal objects lodged in your carcass. After that
they dress you in a pair of those papery hospital PJs, lay you on
a slab and feed you, like an uncooked pizza, into the maw of a
huge machine. "Don't move for the next fifteen minutes," they
tell you. And oh yes, "It will be noisy."

Noisy doesn't cover it. For the next quarter of an hour you
will feel like you've been encased in a corrugated drainpipe and

rolled into the middle of a heavy construction site. You'll hear banging and clanging and buzzing and tweeting. It's so loud they actually fit you out with earmuffs to dampen the sound.

Odd. I'd have thought that being encased in a giant machine that takes snapshots of your body would have been one of the few quiet places left on the planet.

They're getting harder to find, those quiet places. You would think the tiny village of New Denver, BC, deep in the Slocan Valley of the West Kootenays, would be well supplied with oases of tranquility, and in fact it is. And some New Denverites are fighting to keep it that way. A while back the BC telephone company Telus trumpeted the news that it was going to extend cellphone coverage to the town. Yippee. Now everybody in New Denver could be wired into the outside world by cellphone! A Telus spokesman bragged that the impending service was "an economic driver to bring them into the 21st century."

"No thanks," said New Denver.

Bill Roberts of the Slocan Valley Economic Development Commission told a *Vancouver Sun* reporter, "When you're portaging between two lakes and all you're hearing is the call of the loons and the rustles of the forest, the last thing you want to hear is a BEEP BEEP or the opening bars of *Colonel Bogey's March*."

Bill Roberts and friends think not being electronically joined at the ear to the rest of the modern world will be New Denver's touristic ace in the hole. Their community will be one of the few places left in North America—on the planet, in fact—where the cellphone will be useless. "It'll be a big competitive advantage," says Roberts. "We won't have people answering the darned thing everywhere and yelling on it."

Funny how some people can't handle simple peace and quiet. Recently the City of Victoria in BC announced plans to install Aeolian wind harps in one of the city's parks. Hans Schmid fired off a letter to the editor with a basic question—why?

What the park needs, he wrote, is not more but fewer

human-made sounds. "Our public parks should be quiet sanctuaries. If anything, we need more truly tranquil havens."

The odd thing is, Victoria has no problem banning natural sounds. Within the city limits it's perfectly fine for drunks to yodel, airbrakes to screech, horns to honk, car stereos to throb and Aeolian harps to twang—but don't try to keep a rooster.

Bill Murphy made that mistake. As a treat for his kids, he brought home eight day-old chicks, one of which proved to be a rooster. Then he got a knock on the door from an animal control officer. The hens could stay but the rooster had to go. "We had a complaint," she said.

Strange, because Murphy had gone to some lengths to muffle the henhouse and the rooster's early morning calls. Most of the neighbours didn't mind. They loved hearing the cock crow in the morning. Except for one.

The newspaper story prompted another letter to the editor: "It is sad to hear that this rural sound is not welcome in [Victoria]. I am a senior myself and I have heard that the next life is very quiet. I am not in such a rush to get there myself."

Me? I'm lucky enough to live in a rooster-friendly, non-Aeolian-harped neighbourhood. But should I ever have to move, and my choices come down to New Denver or Victoria?

No contest.

USING OUR NURDLES

DEAR DIARY

I never travel without my diary. One should always have something sensational to read on the train.

—Oscar Wilde

Do you keep a diary? Millions do. It's a practice that's been going on for thousands of years. The Paleolithic cave paintings of Lascaux and Altamira are preliterate diaries of a sort, as are the pictograms that adorn stone outcroppings from Queenston, Ontario to Queensland, Australia.

As for the pencil and paper, hide-under-your-pillow diaries—it's hard to say just when that pastime started, but it's had many enthusiastic practitioners. Queen Victoria kept a diary, as did Harry Truman, Ronald Reagan and William Lyon Mackenzie King. (How do you think we found out he channelled his dead mother through his shaving mirror?)

Leaders and losers, heroes and has-beens, our urge to tell the world about ourselves runs wide and deep. Dostoevsky kept a diary. Train-wreck-in-progress rocker-alcoholic Pete Doherty, Franz Kafka and Joseph Goebbels; Andy Warhol and Anne Frank; Buckminster Fuller and Lewis Carroll—diarists all.

Perhaps the most famous diarist was an obscure seventeenth-century British naval bureaucrat named Samuel Pepys. He eventually worked his way up to become chief secretary of the Admiralty and a Member of Parliament, but that's not what he's remembered for.

Pepys is immortal thanks to the meticulous quill-pen-and-parchment diary that he maintained each day for just nine years beginning in 1660. His diary amounts to an eyewitness account—in many cases the only eyewitness account—of momentous events in British history including the Great Plague of London, the Second Dutch War and the Great Fire of London. He also gave us invaluable glimpses into the everyday life of everyday Londoners—sometimes with a waspish turn of phrase: "December 25, 1665. Saw a wedding in the church; and strange to say what delight we married people have to see these poor fools decoyed into our condition."

The great Samuel Johnson, himself the subject of diarist James Boswell, thought highly of the diary habit. "The great thing to be recorded is the state of your own mind," he wrote. "You should write down everything you remember, for you cannot judge at first what is good or bad; and write immediately while the impression is fresh, for it will not be the same a week afterwards."

Write down *everything* you remember? Was Johnson nuts?

Perhaps, but two centuries later, the Reverend Robert Shields of Dayton, Washington, took the old lexicographer at his word. Reverend Shields started his diary in 1972—and spent the next twenty-five years recording his life.

All of it. He spent four hours each day hunched over his diary, recording light bulbs that he changed, junk mail he received and newspaper articles he read. He recorded his body temperature, his blood pressure and his trips to the biffy. In fact he had three dozen ways to describe his urinations.

Reverend Shields also thought it important to keep a record

of his dreams, so he slept in two-hour stretches, the better to write down the dreams while they were still fresh.

Why? Reverend Shields couldn't really explain it. "You might say I'm a nut," he admitted. "We are driven by compulsions we don't know."

And he'll never be able to tell us. Reverend Shields has passed away. He did his very best to record his life, as he lived it, in five-minute segments. And nothing was too trivial: "Sunday August 13, 1995: 9.25-9.35—I dressed in a pair of black Haband trousers, a white mesh shirt, the Haband blue blazer with simulated silver buttons, eyeglasses, the 14-degree Masonic ring, both hearing aids."

In the end he had a work of some 37,500,000 words, all of which he bequeathed to Washington State University with the proviso that no one read it for the next fifty years.

Should anyone want to.

That's one way to keep a diary. France's Louis XVI took a different approach. On July 14, 1789, tens of thousands of enraged Parisians stormed the Bastille, releasing political prisoners being held there. The French Revolution—the biggest political convulsion in the history of that country—had begun.

The French king's diary entry for the day? One word.

"*Rien.*"

EVERYTHING I LEARNED WAS WRONG

I have always been short on coolth. As a child I tripped over the sandbox, coloured outside the lines and did enough face plants off my CCM trike to qualify as a kamikaze in training. As a teen I was a miserable student, a gormless pursuer of the opposite sex and inevitably the very last pick for the baseball team.

Pathetic in the primary grades, hapless in high school, a casualty in college—but I never despaired because I read. I read and read and read.

Not the heavy hitters. No Schopenhauer or Heidelberg. I read the little stuff. Cereal boxes. Labels on mattresses, billboards, Classic Comics books. Eventually I inched my way up to *Life* magazine and *Reader's Digest* and the *Farmers' Almanac*.

Sure, it wasn't terribly elevated material, but at least it made my brain turn over, and it gave me a lot of facts, a lot of newsy nuggets that could help me hopscotch down the crooked, corkscrewed, snakes-and-ladders path of life.

Here are some of the eternal verities I picked up on early:

- The human appendix is a useless organ.

- Everybody should learn mouth-to-mouth respiration.

- You should always bundle up before you go outside in winter.

Wrong, wrong and wrong. Everything I learned was wrong.

When I was a kid, everyone, the school nurse and my doctor included, assured me that the appendix—that slimy little sac in my belly—was a treacherous bag of pus that performed no useful function whatsoever.

"It was different for cavemen," my doctor told me. "They drank out of swamps and ate rancid meat. Their appendixes filtered out and stored the toxins so they couldn't kill them. But in modern man, the little beggar just fills up with poison and sometimes bursts. Better to have it out."

Wrong. Scientists at Duke University School of Medicine have concluded that the appendix actually acts as a "safe house," storing and even cultivating good bacteria essential to human health.

Ironically, one of the reasons we have so many cases of appendicitis these days (321,000 in the US each year) is that the appendix has very little useful to do anymore. Our guts are too clean. It's like having a Formula One racer revving in the garage. Sooner or later it's going to blow a gasket.

As for mouth-to-mouth respiration, since grade nine I've been taught that if someone keels over clutching his chest and turning purple, first thing to do is cardiopulmonary resuscitation (CPR); lock lips and blow some air into them, followed by quick chest compressions. That's still true if the cause of distress is near-drowning, choking or a drug overdose, but if the victim is undergoing a heart attack, mouth-to-mouth might kill before it cures.

Researchers at Tokyo's Surugadai Nihon University Hospital studied 4,068 patients who had suffered cardiac arrests in front of witnesses. The ones who got their chests hand-pumped (a hundred pumps per minute, approximately) without intervening mouth-to-mouth were twice as likely to recover as the ones who got straight CPR. The doctors reckon that because oxygen levels in the blood don't deteriorate for about six minutes after a heart attack, it's more important to get the heart pumping than the lungs wheezing.

Turns out it's a no-brainer anyway. Studies show that 75 percent of people witnessing a heart attack won't risk mouth-to-mouth with a stranger no matter what.

Which brings me to my third and final shibboleth—the one about catching cold. I can still hear dear old Mum hollering at me as I disappeared down the street, "Artie! Come back here and get your scarf! You'll catch your death of cold!"

Sorry, Mum. Not true. Getting cold doesn't cause colds—catching a virus does.

Dr. Paul Donahue, a physician and national newspaper correspondent says flatly "there is no doubt that viruses cause colds and without them, colds don't happen, regardless of weather conditions."

Ironically, writes Dr. Donahue, we might catch more colds in winter precisely because we stay indoors cooped up with other possibly infected people.

That's what Dr. Donahue says and he ought to know. He's a respected, practising physician.

On the other hand, he never met Ruby Black, card-carrying mother.

If the good doctor ever tried any of that "cold weather doesn't cause colds" on Mum, she'd have slapped a toque and strung mittens on him so fast it'd make his stethoscope spin.

CRUEL AND UNUSUAL PUNISHMENT

You're mistaken if you think wrong-doers are
always unhappy. The really professional evil-doers
love it. They're as happy as larks in the sky.

—MURIEL SPARK

I grew up on another planet, a world that bears little relationship to the one I live in now. There were no homeless people or wandering gangs of "hoodies" in my neighbourhood—or in my province, as far as I could see. Kids left their bikes in the driveway, cars and houses were never locked. We played outside unsupervised until the mosquitoes drove us home. Nobody was afraid of the dark, and strangers were just people you hadn't met yet. It was an innocent time and place, where almost nothing horrendous, immoral or illegal ever seemed to happen.

Unless the Hartmans were involved.

The Hartmans—not so much a family as a pagan gang related by blood—lived in a shack to which no one—aside from bill collectors, truancy officers or the occasional constable—ever ventured. It was pretty much the private preserve of Old Man Hartman, Mrs. Hartman and an indeterminate number of grubby kids ranging from toddlers to teenagers. And all of them trouble. The parents drank and threw their beer bottles out in the yard, which was strewn with trash and the cannibalized carcasses of various cars and trucks. The older kids fought, stole bikes and baseball mitts and generally terrorized their peers. The littlest Hartmans stayed in the shadows and tried to survive until they were big enough to make the shift from prey to predator.

The Hartmans partied hard and often, long after the rest of us *Leave It To Beaver* burghers had donned our PJs, sipped our cocoa and gone to bed. They knew that they were hated and feared by their neighbours and they took a fierce, defiant pride in it.

If the Hartmans were around today, they would be labelled as disadvantaged and invested with a succession of court-ordered counsellors, adjudicators and government services to lubricate their re-entry into society.

And they would laugh. In truth they were vicious deadbeats, and those kids would grow up to do time for everything from petty theft to armed robbery and rape. The fact is, society was dumbstruck and gobsmacked by the Hartmans. Nobody had any idea what to do with them. What made it tolerable was the fact that the Hartmans were an anomaly. The rest of the neighbourhood was orderly and decent and, well, bourgeois, so that everything functioned reasonably well.

But as you've probably noticed, there are a lot more Hartmans around today. And we still don't know what to do with them.

In Britain public drunkenness, brawling and general hooliganism are such a problem that the government has taken to handing out ASBOs—anti-social behaviour orders. ASBOs are usually imposed for a term of between two and five years and forbid the subject from harassing or alarming the public. They can also exclude the subject from visiting particular areas of town and from hanging out with other named individuals.

In the Netherlands authorities have gone one step further. They've built special communities for anti-social types—people whose neighbours are fed up with loud, messy, drunken behaviour. The communities are on the outskirts of various towns and strictly monitored.

It's not a life sentence. Anyone who shows that he or she can live responsibly and be respectful of neighbours can earn the right to eventually rejoin society and move back home. Those who don't can party and swear and fight and carouse all they want—under twenty-four-hour supervision.

Interestingly, a lot of people choose Door Number Two. "Lots of people who rebel against noise ordinances or zoning regulations actually choose to move into the special communities," says a Dutch observer. "Some people just don't want to fit in. Why should we force them?"

Personally I think the authorities in Australia have a better solution. There's a car park trouble spot in Rockdale, south of Sydney, that solved its hooligan problem quickly and cheaply.

The car park had been taken over by what the Aussies call hoons—teenaged louts with muscle cars and loud radios. They showed up weekends to drink and brawl and rev the night away. Solution? The authorities set up a sound system and put on back-to-back Barry Manilow CDs at full volume. The hoons fled like cockroaches under a Klieg light.

Hey, I'm all for taking back the neighbourhood . . . but *Mandy? Copacabana?*

There's such a thing as cruel and unusual punishment.

A DOG IS A HAM'S BEST FRIEND

Science ignores things that make life worth living
for the simple reason that beauty, love and so on,
are not measurable quantities and science deals
only with what can be measured.

—ALDOUS HUXLEY

Mr. Huxley was bang on. Science is pretty useless when it comes to measuring immeasurables like beauty and love.

And, it turns out, heroism in dogs.

We all grew up with tales of dog heroism—larger-than-life, smart-as-a-whip canines like Rin Tin Tin and Lassie pulling kiddies out of raging cataracts or barking sleeping families awake to save them from a house fire.

All heart-warming folk legends, but what if they were just that? Legends. Mere myths designed to make us feel warm and fuzzy about our warm and furry friends? Researchers at the University of Western Ontario decided to question the widely held belief that pets—dogs specifically—are capable of understanding emergencies and reacting appropriately.

The researchers designed two experiments. In the first, a dozen owners of twelve different breeds of dog walked their pets through a field. Each owner—on a pre-assigned signal—stopped, clutched his chest, gurgled a bit and fell to the ground.

Rin Tin Tin would know what to do. He'd bark an SOS. Lassie would haul the apparent heart attack victim to a taxi stand. The Littlest Hobo would probably find a phone and dial 911 with his nose.

The twelve dogs in the experiment did next to nothing. Some of them barked a little or nuzzled their owner. The toy poodle did search out a bystander, but curled up in the bystander's lap and went to sleep.

In the second experiment the scientists put the dog owners under a collapsed bookcase, making it look like they were pinned and helpless. The dog owners then cried out to their dogs, telling them to "go and get help."

The twelve dogs checked their owners out. Sniffed around the books some. Not a one of them made any move to go and find assistance.

"I wasn't surprised that they didn't," said Bill Roberts. "It appears that [dogs] don't understand when an emergency has occurred or what to do about it."

Now I can tell you a thing or two about Bill Roberts. He's a psychology professor and co-author of the study that resulted from the two aforementioned experiments. I learned that from the newspaper story, but I can tell you one more thing.

Bill Roberts doesn't own a dog. Or if he does, he hasn't been paying attention.

Of course the dogs didn't react when their owners faked heart attacks or pretended to be helpless under a fallen bookcase. Dogs may or may not be smart enough to go for help in an emergency, but they are definitely smart enough to recognize lousy acting when they see it.

Dogs don't see situations so much as smell them. Real victims of emergencies give off chemical cues that even Christopher Plummer or Meryl Streep couldn't fake.

Those twelve dogs at the University of Western Ontario weren't failing an emergency response experiment, they were evaluating an amateur acting seminar—and giving it a "four paws down" rating.

The best reaction to the experiment appeared in my newspaper a day or two after the article about the non-responsive dogs. It was a letter to the editor from Michelle Poulton of Nanoose Bay, BC:

> Did the researchers consider that dogs understand when people are faking an emergency? I have had dogs as pets for many years. While living on Salt Spring Island in the 1980s, I had two dogs, a terrier-cross lab and a coon hound. They were dear but not the smartest bricks in the load. They were trained never to stray on the roads, which were twisty with blind corners.
>
> One day Nipper and Boomer didn't respond to my calls. Then Nipper appeared at the top of the driveway, refusing to come in. I followed him and found a small child tottering down the middle of the windy, dangerous road.
>
> On either side of him were my two wonderful dogs.

To which I can only add, "Amen, Michelle."

And Professor Roberts? You still have a lot to learn.

Get yourself a dog.

I FORGIVE YOU, MISS SANFORD

They say that back in the days of the Korean War the first four English words any Korean kid living in the war zone mastered were, "Hey, Joe—got gum?"

That's because (a) our soldiers were easy marks and (b) they always had lots of chewing gum to share. Military leaders like to keep soldiers well supplied with gum. They think that aside from being a mini-treat, gum relieves stress and keeps the doughboys alert.

This was one of my early lessons in the inherent unfairness of life, because back in the fifties when foreign kids were walking around chewing great gobs of free gum in Korea, my teacher, Miss Sanford, was thwacking me across the knuckles with a yardstick for doing the same thing in her grade five class.

Chewing gum was a no-no in our classrooms and understandably so, I guess. In my early academic career, I left my share of well-chewed stalactites cemented to the underside of a succession of school desks. Teachers didn't cotton to kids who chewed gum in class. Janitors who had to chisel off our deposits must have really hated us.

Funny stuff, chewing gum. Most people assume it's a North American phenomenon, but ancient Greeks had the habit too. They chewed a gummy resin they scraped off the bark of the mastic tree, which in fact is where our verb "masticate" comes from. A few hundred years later the ancient Mayans took up chewing the coagulated sap of the sapodilla tree. They called their chaw of choice chicle.

Around 1850 a Yankee entrepreneur by the name of Thomas Adams imported a batch of the sap and ripped off the name while he was at it, which is how we ended up with Adams Chiclets.

PR-wise it's been an uphill battle for chewing gum. Teachers and janitors have always deplored it. Puritanical types considered it a morale-sapping addiction. Some gloomy-Gus physicians cautioned that chewing too much gum would dry up our salivary glands. But the tide is slowly turning, and chewing gum is finally getting some good press. Experts now allow that there's an upside to the gum habit. We know that chewing gum during airplane flights can give respite from painful earaches caused by changing air pressure. We've learned that sugar-free gum helps to neutralize stomach acidity. Now a cancer researcher by the name of Julie Sharp says that chewing gum helps patients recovering from intestinal surgery by kick-starting the digestive tract. Chewing gum, she says, is a cheap and simple procedure that can get patients back on their feet in record time.

Still not convinced that chewing gum is good for you? Tell it to Frank Cauley.

That would be Flight Officer (Retired) Frank Cauley of the RCAF. On March 10, 1944, Cauley and his crew were aloft in a Sunderland flying boat over the North Atlantic when they caught a German U-boat on the surface, scrambling to submerge. They attacked, swooping in to within fifty feet of the sub before they dropped their depth charges. They sank the sub, but not without a fight. The Sunderland was shuddering as a result of major structural damage from the U-boat's anti-aircraft gun. "We sustained a big hole in the bow of the plane," remembers Cauley, "and about three dozen smaller shrapnel holes."

They used up all their emergency leak stoppers filling the gaping rupture in the bow, but the remaining thirty-odd small holes were worrisome. The Sunderland was a flying boat, which meant sooner or later it had to land on the water. Those small, unpatched holes could put them all at the bottom of the sea.

You know where this is going, don't you?

Remember what I said about the military and chewing gum? It applies to the Canadian military too. Frank Cauley was one of a crew of eleven on that Sunderland. Each of them carried—on each mission and as a matter of course—a ration of five sticks of Wrigley's spearmint gum.

As the Sunderland bucketed along, the whole crew started chewing. Hard.

"Fifty-five sticks of gum later," recalls Cauley, "we had plugged the shrapnel holes with gum. We went up to 3,000 feet where the gum froze."

After that it was a breeze. They all made it back safely to their home base in Castle Archdale, Northern Ireland.

And Flight Officer (Retired) Frank Cauley, RCAF, has carried a single stick of Wrigley's in his pocket ever since.

Don't blame him.

Miss Sanford? Did you catch that?

MOTTO MADNESS

I'm feeling just a smidgen of sympathy for somebody I don't even know. This nameless functionary is probably toiling in the bowels of the Manitoba government as I speak. He or she is the beleaguered bureaucrat responsible for coming up with Manitoba's brand new provincial motto, which is—deep breath now:

"Spirited Energy."

That's it. Somebody—more likely a committee—stood back and looked at Manitoba's 650,000 square kilometres of lakes and rivers, boundless flatlands and majestic rolling hills, took into consideration its million-plus inhabitants and the rich tapestry of historical figures including everyone from Neil Young to Tommy Douglas, from Marshall McLuhan to Deanna Durbin . . .

And came up with "Spirited Energy."

Not surprisingly, Manitobans reacted with spirited, energetic expressions of disbelief and dismay. John Gleeson, a *Winnipeg Sun* columnist wrote, "The first thing that struck me about the phrase is that it hardly rolls off the tongue. Try saying it three times and you might choke to death. The next thing I realized about the slogan is that it really sucks."

Which is true, but perhaps a little hard on the unfortunate wretch or wretches who coined the even more unfortunate phrase. After all, most of Canada's provincial mottos—er—suck, as it were.

Take Nova Scotia's motto, for example. *Spem reduxit,* it proclaims in a language that no one has spoken seriously for a couple of thousand years. It means approximately, "Hope was restored."

Oh? Had someone stolen it? Has anyone told the Mounties?

Then there's British Columbia's motto, *Splendor sine occasu.* That translates as "Splendour without diminishment."

A pretty sentiment, I suppose, although more than a tad lofty for a chunk of terrestrial geography that gave the world Brother Twelve, Pamela Anderson and Bill Vander Zalm.

Alberta's motto *Fortis et liber* (Strong and free) is, if nothing else, as blunt and straightforward as Ralph Klein after his eighth beer.

And Quebec's motto—what was that again? Oh yeah, I remember—*Je me souviens.*

It also illustrates that government-mandated mottos don't have to be in Latin. Montana's no-nonsense, follow-the-money motto is in Spanish. *Oro y plata* means "Gold and silver."

The state of Maryland has an Italian motto: *Fatti maschi, parole femmine.*

It means "Manly deeds, womanly words."

Perhaps something was lost in translation . . .

But I think the most unfortunate geographical motto belongs to South Carolina. *Dum spiro spero,* it proclaims.

Which translates better than it sounds. In English it means "While I breathe, I hope."

Unfortunately, it reads like a searing indictment of President Richard Nixon's infamously felonious veep, Spiro Agnew.

But South Carolina, Maryland, New Brunswick—yea, even spiritedly energetic Manitoba—can all take solace in one indisputable consolation.

At least they ain't Joisey.

That state recently asked its citizens to come up with a new state motto to replace the stale and slightly pompous "Liberty and prosperity." Six thousand New Jerseyites responded. Many of the submissions were dignified and noble, but several were obviously written with tongue in cheek and with references to New Jersey's reputation for pollution—both environmental and political.

"Come to New Jersey," one suggestion read, "We can always use another relative on the payroll."

Another one said, "New Jersey: it's not as bad as it smells."

And my favourite was the Tony Soprano-tinged, "You want a $%#@* motto? I got yer *&^%$#@ motto right here!"

Hey! There's a motto for Manitoba.

"Friendly Manitoba: it's way better than New Jersey, eh?"

SOUNDS GOOD TO ME

van Hogarth was the town bully where I grew up. A vicious little bugger built like a fire hydrant and with the personality of a pit bull with a toothache.

Tough too. He cornered each of us and thumped us out at one time or another, including some kids three or four years his senior.

I was no match for Ivan and I knew it. I stayed away from the street he lived on and the corner of the schoolyard he considered his kingdom. If I saw him coming, I dropped whatever I was doing and ran like a gazelle.

Except for one day a year. There was always at least one day each winter when I went looking for Ivan. It would be right after a fresh snowfall, and the temperature would be cold—cold enough to make the snow crunch under my feet with every step.

That's when I went after Ivan like a peregrine falcon power-diving on a partridge. If I was lucky enough to find him, I'd go right up to him and say, "Hey, Hogarth! Check this out!" And I would execute a crisp tarantella, stomping my snow boots like a Gypsy dancer on methedrine.

And Ivan Hogarth would clutch his ears, fall to the ground and writhe. He couldn't stand the sound of crunching snow. It disabled him.

That was Ivan's least favourite sound, which automatically made it one of my favourites. What about you? What sound drives you batty?

For many folks it's some variation of a scraping noise, the classic being fingernails dragged across a blackboard. Even Aristotle grumbled about "the aversive quality" of certain objects scraping against each other.

Other "aural-sensitives" complain about the sound of cats in heat or wailing babies, neither of which will ever be confused with a Mozart sonata.

My partner claims that "loud snoring" is the most repulsive sound for her. (Which frankly, makes me somewhat suspicious. Where is she getting this stuff? I know that I certainly don't snore . . .)

But that's her acoustical hang-up. The truth is, there's not a lot of agreement on what is the worst sound in the world. And if there's one sound that investigator Trevor Cox can't stand, it's the sound of silence. Professor Cox is a professor of engineering at the University of Salford in England. Recently he made it his mission to identify, isolate and make public the all-time, no-question-about-it very worst noise a human can hear. He embarked on a year-long online study that consisted pretty much of just one question:

What sound bugs you the most?

Professor Cox offered a short list of thirty-four hideous sounds to choose from. More than one million people responded.

Surprisingly nails on a blackboard didn't even place in the top ten. It came in sixteenth, just before the sound of a polystyrene coffee cup being scrunched.

Other major revolting sounds: the whine of a dentist's drill, the inanity of cellphone ring tones and microphone feedback. "Hello? Can you hear me? Is this thing on? SCREEEEEEAWRRRRRRRRRRRRRRRK. Oh. Sorry."

And the number-one worst sound? The one noise most people identify as uniquely unbearable?

A person vomiting.

Pretty gross, all right, but I wouldn't call it the worst sound in the world. Still, one person's caterwaul is another person's music of the spheres. Samuel Johnson, the world's most famous lexicographer and one of the grumpiest men ever to voice an opinion, once sat through a harpsichord solo performed by a noted artist. When she had finished and Johnson had said nothing, the harpsichordist enquired daintily as to whether Mr. Johnson was "fond of music."

"No, Madame," groused the curmudgeon, "but of all noises I think music is the least disagreeable."

The worst sound for me? It's a hard choice. Nails on a blackboard don't bother me. Crying babies can be somewhat annoying, but not what I'd call excruciating. I think the sound that most gets to me is some nasally challenged stranger sniffing continuously. I usually get one of them behind me in the theatre or next to me in the waiting room. I can't count the number of times I've entertained fantasies of violent homicide when a couple of Kleenexes would have solved the problem.

Yeah. That's my number one least favourite sound: a sniffler.

But snow crunching underfoot? Ah. That's still music to my ears.

A GREASY MIRACLE

My old man was a wonderful guy—kind, generous, funny and sweet. But he had one habit that creeped us all out.

He ate a spoonful of Vaseline every day.

Vaseline. Petroleum jelly. The goop you smear on babies' bums to prevent diaper rash. Gaaaaaaaack!

Not to knock the product—I doubt there's a medicine cabinet in Canada that doesn't contain a tube or a jar of the stuff—but it's for putting on rashes and scrapes and cuts. It's not intended for shoving down your cakehole.

An odd unguent is Vaseline, when you think about it: cheap, odourless and a century and a half old. We can thank a British-born American chemist by the name of Robert Augustus Chesebrough for Vaseline. Way back in 1859, while touring some oil rigs in Pennsylvania, Chesebrough noticed some sticky, smelly goop adhering to the drilling rods. "We call it rod wax," a roughneck told him. "Great for cuts and burns." Chesebrough scooped up a canful and took it back to his shop.

Ten years later, he'd managed to get rid of the stinky, sticky components and was left with the colourless, odourless gel we all know today. "Eureka!" thought Chesebrough. He named it Vaseline, combining the German word for water and the Greek word for oil. Then he waited for the orders to start flowing in.

They didn't. American pharmacists couldn't have cared less about Chesebrough's new wonder jelly. He couldn't even give the stuff away.

It was the era of snake-oil salesmen, and Chesebrough adopted snake-oil selling tactics. He went on the road with a chuckwagon full of Vaseline. Wherever he could draw a crowd, he would deliberately hold his hand over a candle flame, jab himself with a penknife or even pour muriatic acid on his arm. When he had a nice, raw wound going, he would slather on some Vaseline and assure the crowd that the pain had disappeared and his wound would be healed by the next day. Then he'd hand out free but tiny samples. "Where can we get some more?" the crowds asked.

"Go to your pharmacist," Chesebrough told them. "Ask for it by name. Vaseline." They did, and pretty soon the orders were pouring in. Chesebrough was on his way to being a very wealthy, if somewhat scarred, man.

The irony is, Vaseline isn't really any good at curing cuts, scratches and burns. Medical researchers have determined that Vaseline has no curative power whatsoever. What a layer of Vaseline does is keep bacteria out of the wound, which in turn helps it to heal faster than it normally would. Doctors call it an occlusive moisturizer. It creates a barrier on the skin while keeping the skin moist and supple.

But that's just the beginning of the miracle of Vaseline. Got a vintage baseball mitt that's all dried out? Slather it with Vaseline to make it soft again.

Are you fed up with the way those dinky outdoor Christmas light bulbs get jammed in their sockets? Rub a thin coat of Vaseline on the threads before inserting the bulbs.

Want to avoid paint splatters when you're redecorating a room? Swab some Vaseline around the edges of door hinges, doorknobs, locks, anything you don't want paint on. Any paint that lands on the Vaseline wipes off with a clean cloth.

Want to prevent that buildup of ugly crud that likes to accumulate on the top of your car battery? Smear some you-know-what on the terminals. The battery will still work like a charm and it won't look like the Great Barrier Reef when you open the hood.

Hell, you can even catch fish with Vaseline. Just cut up a sponge into little pieces, coat them with Vaseline and thread them onto your hook. Fish will be suckered into thinking they've found a blob of tasty fish eggs.

And it goes without saying that Vaseline is excellent for diaper rash, chapped lips, rashes and chafes.

It must be doing something right—fifteen million jars sell every year.

But I draw the line at eating the stuff. In fact I've only heard of one person in the world other than my old man who indulged in that practice.

Robert Augustus Chesebrough. Ate a teaspoon every single morning of his entire adult life.

Died at the age of 96.

Makes you think.

GLADSOME GLEANINGS
FROM THE GL GLOSSARY

don't make a habit of rhapsodizing over the juxtaposition of two of the twenty-six letters in our alphabet, but lately I've been gleefully gloating over the glut of glorious words that would fit in the *gl* glossary.

If there was a *gl* glossary.

It's quite striking, the number—and power—of English words that begin with (or contain) the *gl* combination.

Like, for instance, "English."

It's a construction that gives us beautiful words like "globular" and "glissando" and "gladiola."

It spawns plenty of powerful, evocative words as well. Words like "glower," "glaze" and "glitter." It also serves up its share of ugly (there it is again) words like "glutton" and "gloat" and "glitch." We've even, in our lifetimes, imported a Russian *gl* word—"glasnost."

In his book *Welcome to the Monkey House*, Kurt Vonnegut went so far as to coin a brand new *gl* word. Are you familiar with that horrible, lifeless brown-green slop that coats the bottom of harbours and bays polluted by too many boats and unhouse-broken humans? Vonnegut was too. He dubbed the toxic slime "glurp."

Mr. Vonnegut is no longer with us, more's the pity, but I have a feeling he would approve of two brand new *gl* words lately, ahem, "gleaned" from our ubiquitous friend the internet.

The first is "glamping." Glamping is what happens when Paris Hilton meets Lord Baden-Powell. The word is a contraction of two words that you'd think would form a natural oxymoron—glamour and camping. Glampers are people who enjoy the beauty and peace of the great outdoors but not the hardships associated with actually, you know, experiencing it. They don't care for lumpy sleeping bags, smoky campfires, leaky tents or pungent pit toilets. When one goes glamping, one avoids all that awkward, messy back-to-nature stuff. Glampers luxuriate in capacious tents with real beds, duvets and even Persian-carpeted floors. These tents, which would do a Saudi oil sheik proud, come with power outlets, the better to provide electric light and juice to run those oh-so-necessary PlayStations, BlackBerrys and hair dryers.

Don't look for these pastoral palaces to be springing up in campgrounds at Banff or Algonquin Park or even the local KOA trailer park—at least not yet. So far the fad of glamping is pretty much confined to Europe, where upscale glampers like Kate Moss and Sienna Miller glamorized the practice by showing up at music festivals and demanding five-star treatment.

They definitely started something. Marks & Spencer, the British retail store, has just announced a whole new line of fancy-pants tents and glamping accessories including floral tent pegs.

Floral tent pegs. Can you imagine what Grey Owl would say?

It may be largely a European phenomenon so far, but there

are signs that it's already made a North American landfall. A report in the *Los Angeles Times* notes that although the overall number of visitors to US national parks is dropping, sporadic flocks of glampers have begun to raise their well-coiffed heads.

But I promised you two new *gl* words, didn't I? Okay, here's the second one:

"Glurge."

Don't know what it means? Check your email. Chances are you've got two or three examples of glurge in your inbox. The online *Urban Dictionary* has the best definition I've read.

Glurge: Word used to describe the syrupy sweet emails that are mass-mailed to unwilling participants. Usually involve, puppies, kitties, children with disabilities, puppies and kitties with disabilities, and Jesus. Generally end with, "Pass this along 2 as many ppl as u can!!!!!!"

Yep, we've all seen too many of those.

But here's a thought. What if a couple of Glaswegian glampers—say Glenn Close and Gary Glitter—gleefully gathered in a glen near Glastonbury to glue together a conglomeration of glittering glurges, then wangled a single-access website where they could dangle their new-fangled jingles for all the world to see?

That would be glorious. And something we could all glom onto.

TOO DUMB TO BE TRUE

Just got a beauty email. "PLEEEEEEASE REEEEAD THIS!" the subject line screams, "IT WAS ON THE GOOD MORNING AMERICA SHOW . . ."

The accompanying email explains that, for every person I forward the message to, Microsoft will send me a cheque for $245. For every third person that receives it, Bill Gates will see that I get a cheque for $241.

Why would Microsoft do that? Because they're running "an email beta test," says the sender.

Oh, of course. An email beta test.

There are only two valid philosophical responses to an email like this: "Yeah." And "Right."

Hard to believe there are sentient humans out there credulous enough to fall for something as palpably phony as this. Still it does help to explain how George Bush got elected twice.

Okay, once.

It also helps to explain the continuing popularity of urban legends. You know—modern folklore—wildly improbable stories that travel at the speed of light, precisely because the people who tell them are so utterly convinced they're gospel. Most often the teller insists that the event happened to a cousin's boyfriend or an uncle's ex-wife or a "friend of a friend."

That's why a lot of urban legend collectors refer to these tales as FOAFs—Friend-of-a-Friend stories.

You know the ones I mean. Stories about a woman poisoned by spiders nesting in her beehive hairdo. Stories about cement-filled Cadillacs, microwaved chihuahuas and kids decapitated by a ceiling fan while jumping on a hotel bed.

Never happened—any one of them. Simple common sense would tell you that.

And how about that totally ridiculous story of Larry, the guy who attached forty-two helium balloons to an aluminum lawn chair in his girlfriend's backyard, and armed with a six-pack and a pellet pistol, soared to nearly five thousand metres over Los Angeles? The story claimed he stayed aloft for an hour and a half and was spotted in flight by the pilots of at least two airliners. Legend had it that Larry executed a controlled descent by shooting out selected helium balloons with his air pistol. But only after his feet started to get cold.

Can you believe anyone in the world could be gullible enough to fall for a tall tale like that?

Well . . . actually, folks, that one is true.

Outlandish as it sounds, there was a guy—a Los Angeles truck driver named Larry Walters—who on July 2, 1982, actually did all of the above and lived to talk about it on the *David Letterman Show*. He almost didn't make it. Some of his balloons got snarled in power lines and caused a blackout in an LA residential neighbourhood. Larry could have been quite literally toast, but his lawn chair cleared the lines and he came in for a three-point landing.

Officers from the Federal Aviation Agency were waiting for him. They'd never had to deal with a flying lawn chair before, but they improvised brilliantly. Walters was charged with "reckless operation of an aircraft," "failure to stay in communication with the tower" and—my favourite—"flying a civil aircraft for which there is not currently in effect an airworthiness certificate." They dinged him fifteen hundred bucks for his little adventure.

Could have been worse. Could have been like Patrick Lawrence, a twenty-seven-year-old unemployed drywaller who was arrested in a pumpkin patch on the outskirts of Macon, Georgia, a couple of years ago. The charge: public intoxication, public indecency, and also lewd and lascivious behaviour.

The reality: Patrick Lawrence was arrested for . . . having his way . . . with a pumpkin.

As the arresting officer, Brenda Taylor, explained it, "I just went up to [Lawrence] and said, 'Excuse me sir, but do you realize that you are . . . involved with a pumpkin?'"

At which the drunken Lawrence looked up and said, "A pumpkin? Damn . . . is it midnight already?"

True story? Of course not. But possibly a sign that urban legends are developing a sense of humour.

USING OUR NURDLES

Know what a nurdle is? You should. We're pumping five and a half quadrillion of them into the environment each year. They'll all be around for the next five hundred years.

Nurdles are grains, granules, kernels, pellets of that most familiar of modern-day materials, plastic. An amazing phenomenon, plastic. We've only been producing the stuff on a large scale for fifty-odd years, yet already it permeates every stratum of our lives. Our clothes are increasingly made of plastic; our cars and airplanes and boats are largely plastic. So are our cellphones, our credit cards, our sunglasses and our artificial heart valves.

I'm typing these words on a plastic keyboard.

Billions of items that were once made out of metal or wood are now plastic. But unlike aluminum or cedar, plastic doesn't degrade when we're finished with it. Of all the billions of tons of plastic we've produced in the past half-century, not one nurdle of it has died a natural death. A tiny fraction has been incinerated—transformed into a different, less visible form of pollution—but the rest is still with us in landfill sites and vacant lots.

But mostly in our oceans. One time I met a woman who had travelled all over the world. Tell me the most amazing thing you ever saw, I said. She didn't even hesitate. "On the shores of the Red Sea," she said, "I looked down from a hill one morning at dawn and saw thousands—millions—of ghostly white, blue, green and yellow creatures wafting across the sand away from the water, as far as the eye could see."

What were they, I asked—storks? Flamingos? Seagulls?

"Plastic bags," she said. They had washed up on the shore, dried out in the sun and begun to migrate who knows where.

About sixteen hundred kilometres off the coast of California there's an undulating blob of bags and other plastic crap going round and round and round. It is the size of two New Brunswicks. It will rotate out there for centuries after you and I are dead.

It's a wonder we aren't buried in plastic bags. We manufacture five hundred billion of the things, a million every minute, each year. And we throw them all away, except they refuse to *go* away—they stay—and the damage they do is nigh incalculable. The discarded plastic bags that make their way into our waters wreak havoc with ocean life. Sea turtles mistake them for their favourite food, jellyfish. They eat the bags and die. Dolphins, porpoises and a host of sea creatures think they're seaweed and gulp them down. What's really sad is that plastic bags are a frill, a sop to our sloth and thoughtlessness. We could easily bring our own reusable cloth bags to the grocery store. Broccoli doesn't care how it gets from the checkout counter to the refrigerator.

Happily there seems to be a grassroots revolt growing against this most disposable and despicable form of plastics pollution. Filmmaker Rebecca Hosking caused a mini-revolution in a small town in England. Hosking had spent a year filming life—and death—on the beaches of Hawaii. When she returned to her home town of Modbury, she set up a local screening of her film and invited the town's forty-three shopkeepers to attend. "Come and see where the plastic bags you hand out end up," she told them. They saw sea turtles gasping and choking on plastic bags. They saw dolphins belly up in the surf and sea birds enmeshed in plastic. When the film was done and the lights came up, Hosking asked for a show of hands in support of a voluntary ban on plastic bags. Unanimous. And Modbury became the first town in Europe to be plastic-bag-free.

Other jurisdictions are taking action too. Ireland slapped a "plas tax" on all plastic bags sold in the country. The tax not only raised millions of euros that were subsequently channelled toward environmental projects, it also reduced the use of plastic bags in Ireland by an astonishing 95 percent.

Several years ago Hong Kong called for a voluntary ban on plastic-bag use. In its first year Hong Kong supermarkets handed out eighty million fewer plastic bags.

When you think of it, it's all voluntary in the end. If we wait for our trudging, begrudging, snail-paced governments to act, we'll be up to our Adam's apples in plastic.

So what to say when the check-out clerk asks, "Paper or plastic?"

Not "Plastic," for sure—but chopping down a tree to produce a grocery bag seems like a pretty Faustian bargain too.

How about "Neither, thanks—I brought my own bags"?

TAKE CARE OF YOURSELF, Y'HEAR?

Don Hewitt is one smart cookie. He's an eight-time Emmy award winner and creator of *60 Minutes*, the longest-running prime-time broadcast on North American television at forty-plus years and counting. Hewitt's an unquestioned success story and an acknowledged media genius, but even he must jackknife up in bed some nights wincing at the sentence that tumbled out of his mouth back in 1959.

He was interviewing prospective television hosts for the Columbia Broadcasting System and he didn't see much promise in the blonde hopeful sitting across from him waiting for his verdict on her audition. She had a speech impediment—a lisp—for crying out loud.

"With your voice," he told her bluntly, "nobody is going to let you broadcast."

The dumpee handled the rejection well. She walked across the street and signed on with NBC. Her name was Barbara Walters.

That's the secret to handling rejection. Learn to roll with it; don't take it personally. It's an important skill to master, because in this life we all get dumped sooner or later: left at the altar, jilted, fired, sold out, passed over for promotion, selected last for the volleyball team. "It's a long lane that has no ash cans," said John Diefenbaker, a man who knew a thing or two about getting dumped.

Me? I've got enough rejection slips to paper the Rogers Centre, but so have most writers I know. And it helps to know that George Orwell had his book *Animal Farm* rejected out of hand by his American publisher because, as the publisher explained, "It's impossible to sell animal stories in the USA."

The challenge is not just to roll with the punches but to get up and KO the clown who decked you. To rise again, as the great Stan Rogers anthem *Mary Ellen Carter* advises. The real trick is turning pratfalls into pirouettes.

I've never been much good at it, but Sophie Calle is the Karen Kain of rejection revenge. Calle is a fifty-four-year-old Parisian writer, photographer and installation artiste. Last year she got a Dear Jane—make that a *Chère Jeanne*—letter from the guy she was seeing. Not even a letter, an email! It was classic Dumpsville. He was leaving her "for her own good" he wrote. He had found himself "noticing other women" and didn't want to break his promise not to cheat on her, so he was pulling the plug, bailing out, hitting the road. "Take care of yourself," he signed off.

Sophie Calle could have pulled out her hair and sobbed and wailed and gnashed her teeth. She could have called up her girlfriends and boo-hooed with them into the night over bottles of *vin ordinaire*. She had a better idea. She would "take care of herself" all right. She would take care of Monsieur Snake-in-the-Grass *aussi*.

First she made copies of the email. A lot of copies. She mailed them off to professional women she knew, each with a different area of expertise. She sent one photocopy to a copy editor, another to a forensic psychiatrist, another to a professional clown, still another to an opera diva. "Comments? Observations? Advice?" prompted Calle.

The diva sang the letter as a wretchedly cheesy aria. The clown interpreted the letter as a slapstick routine. The forensic shrink diagnosed the mental state of the writer of the letter (not healthy). The copy editor slashed and corrected it with coloured highlighter pens, pointing out the clichés, the misspellings, the bad grammar.

Mme Calle wasn't finished. She called in favours from famous actresses—Jeanne Moreau and Vanessa Redgrave included—and recorded their renditions and comments on camera. She had the letter encrypted as a crossword by a cruciverbalist. She had it evaluated for religious content by a pair of Talmudic scholars. She even persuaded a female marksman to pin the letter to a target in a firing range and shred it with rounds from a high-calibre sniper's rifle.

All in all Sophie Calle shared her ignominious email with 107 female professionals, then photographed and videotaped their responses and interpretations. She put the results—photos, blow-ups of the letter, videotapes—on the walls of the French pavilion of the Venice Biennale art exhibition in a spectacular art installation called (c'est si bon) *Take Care of Yourself*.

The result? Laughter. Peals and peals of cathartic, healing laughter.

A very funny Canadian by the name of Bernie Slade once said, "Laughter is the opposite of a breakdown. It's a breakup." Mme Calle's installation broke up the spectators at the Venice Biennale this summer. It exposed her ex-beau as a none-too-bright, unprincipled sleazeball of the first water and showed Mme Calle to be one very witty, resilient artist.

Who unquestionably knows how to take care of herself.

YOUR ROVING ROBOREPORTER

COME BACK, OLIVE ...
ALL IS FORGIVEN

Does anybody remember life before home computers?

Man, I dated myself right there, didn't I? Nobody talks about home computers anymore. We speak of laptops, notebooks, iPhones and BlackBerrys, but not home computers. That's like talking about home refrigerators or home televisions. Nowadays pretty much everybody this side of a monastery or a Mennonite farmhouse has at least one computer in their lives and in their houses.

For better or worse.

I've been thinking fond and nostalgic thoughts of the girl I ditched about twenty years ago. Sweet thing. Her name was Olive.

Olivetti.

She was my typewriter. A manual portable that I lugged all across Canada and the States plus a good chunk of England, France and Spain. Olive was no beauty—especially after she took that tumble off the roof of my station wagon at ninety-five kilometres an hour. And she was limited, unlike the hot little number I ditched her for. Olive couldn't spell-check, make copies, change fonts, play solitaire or hook me up with the internet, but she was reliable in her own hopelessly old-fashioned way. And she had one virtue that I took for granted at the time. A virtue that I will never enjoy again.

Olive didn't require a password.

I have probably twelve computer passwords in my life. Maybe more; I've no doubt forgotten a few. I have one password for my library, another password for the *Globe and Mail* online. Still others will connect me to the *New York Times*, the Royal Canadian Legion, *Salon* magazine and several online clubs and organizations I am loosely affiliated with.

The question is, why?

Why do I need a password to go online and read a newspaper? Or to check my frequent flyer points? Or to find out when the meat draw is coming up at the Legion? Sure, if I was doing online banking, I suppose I would want the security of my own password—but I don't do online banking. Whenever I get the urge to visit my overdraft, I walk down to the bank and interact with actual breathing, talking human beings.

Why not? They've got soft couches, free coffee and some of the sweetest people in town.

We're living in an age of password paranoia. Cybergeeks have terrorized us into believing that choosing a password has to be as complicated as a nuclear missile launch. Planning to use your middle name followed by your birth year? Forget it—first thing hackers look for. Ditto for using your mother's maiden name, your partner's nickname or any combination involving the name of your dog, your cat or your cockatoo.

Some other advice from these fiends: don't use the same password for everything. Always choose a different one.

Oh yes, and be sure to change all your passwords every few weeks.

As for how to come up with a safe password, the experts advise against using any recognizable words . . . in any language on the face of the earth. Choose a meaningless string of letters and numbers in capitals and lower case, they say.

Swell. So I come up with GwiSN#ARM*filg*//niTR07.

Now how am I supposed to remember that?

I never will, of course. Which is why GwiSN#ARM*filg*// niTR07 is printed out in painstaking ballpoint and attached to my computer screen on a sticky note.

Some security. Anybody with a pair of eyeballs can find out my password by strolling past my desk.

I admit I'm a bit of a password curmudgeon, but I'm not as bad as my buddy Al.

He's a real Luddite—and guaranteed to go postal at the mention of computer passwords. I'm also a bit worried that— how to put this politely?—Al's personal floppy disk may be full. I ran into him down at the coffee shop last week, hunched over his laptop, cursing steadily under his breath.

"This **&@*$X!^#ing program won't let me in without a password," he growled. "Has to be at least seven characters long."

"Heck, that's not bad, Al," I said. "Just seven characters. That's fairly simple as passwords go."

Al says, "Yeah, but look at how long it's gonna be! So far I've come up with Homer Simpson, Carrie Bradshaw, George Costanza, Carmen Soprano, Jack Bauer . . ."

LIFE: IT'S A RISKY BUSINESS

My, it's been a quiet summer in our neighbourhood. I drive by the baseball diamond each afternoon, and there's nobody there. Passing the school track I occasionally spot the odd jogger and maybe one or two old duffers like myself walking their dogs. I hardly ever see any kids.

I remember my prepubescent summers. They were chock-a-block with kids running, biking and lollygagging every which way. Spontaneous baseball games, hanging out at the corner store, riding our bikes around the schoolyard, heading off to the bush to climb trees, scoop frogs and throw rocks. We played catch, tag and touch football and flew kites—a few diehards even dug out their sticks for a game of road hockey—with the sound of "heat bugs" zinging in the trees. On really hot afternoons we trekked down to the swimming hole for a dip, purloined bath towels slung over our shoulders. Back then Canada's population was only about half what it is now.

So where are all the kids hiding?

Answer? Take your pick. Hunched over a computer,

fiddling with Xboxes, watching *Survivor* reruns or down in the basement hooked up to their intravenous iPods.

According to Mary Rivkin, associate professor of education at the University of Maryland, kids just aren't spending as much time outdoors as they used to.

"We're afraid of being outside because of strangers, sun and insects," says Professor Rivkin. Besides, she says, "Outside play takes lots of supervision."

We were too stupid to know that back in my day. In our brute ignorance we just went ahead and played by ourselves. I don't recall any instructors or strangers. As for sun and insects, we basked in one and collected the other in jam jars. We considered free sunshine and weird bugs to be two of the best reasons for being outside in the first place. But we don't trust Mother Nature enough to leave her alone with our kids anymore. When we teach youngsters about the birds and bees nowadays, it's not about procreation, it's about West Nile virus and anaphylactic shock.

Speaking of threats, real and perceived, the next time you're at your local swimming pool, think twice before you try a one-and-a-half gainer off the diving board.

It might not be there.

According to the *Wall Street Journal*, diving boards are being removed from swimming pools all across the US, and new pools are being built without them.

Too dangerous? Nah. Lots of people are injured in swimming pools across North America every year, but surprisingly few of the injuries involve diving boards. Trouble is, the ones that do, also involve lawyers. US legal beagles representing injured divers—or people injured by divers—routinely win damages of five million dollars or more. It's a brave pool owner who will okay a diving board with that threat flutter-kicking in the wings.

You have to wonder just how cocooned the fear mongers

would have us be. Did you know it is now illegal to feed pigeons in London's Trafalgar Square? Drop a sunflower seed near Nelson's Column, and you'll have coppers on your case faster than you can say Bobby's your uncle. "Public hygiene" is the official explanation.

Amazing the British Empire held out against pigeon poo as long as it did, I guess.

It was an Englishman—Sir Noël Coward—who wrote the famous line, "Mad dogs and Englishmen go out in the midday sun," but we've all been cured of that. Nowadays we treat the sun as if it was some rogue nuclear reactor. We don gloves and floppy hats and lather up in sunscreen to protect ourselves from it.

Which brings us to the latest red alert: sunscreen. Seems that nanotechnology (the science of mucking around with sub-atomic particles) has produced a flock of microscopic additives that scientists have been enthusiastically shovelling into new products like sunscreen. One such additive—the titanium dioxide nanoparticle, which is used to block and absorb sunlight—has been found to cause brain damage in laboratory mice. Does it have the same effect on humans? Nobody knows yet. But a scientist with the US Environmental Protection Agency says, "The general message is that we should take these results seriously and be very careful with nanoparticles."

So what's your pleasure: no sunscreen and skin cancer? Or sunscreen and brain damage?

A funny guy named Kevin James says, "I discovered I scream the same way whether I'm about to be devoured by a Great White or if a piece of seaweed touches my foot."

Same here, Kevin. I think we all need to work on recognizing the difference.

TAKE ME OUT TO
THE SHELL GAME

Consider the humble baseball.

Not much to it—just a swatch of horsehide stitched around a ball of cork and twine innards. You can go out and buy one for about $7.99 plus tax.

Unless said baseball is signed by the guy who last belted it out of the park. Then you might pay thousands, even millions of dollars, for the privilege of ownership.

It's crazy but it's true. Charlie Sheen, the actor, paid over US$93,500 for the infamous baseball that Bill Buckner bobbled in game six of the 1986 World Series. The first ball Babe Ruth knocked over the wall of Yankee Stadium sold for 130 grand. Mickey Mantle's five-hundredth home run ball went for a quarter of a million bucks.

Who pays this kind of money for a lousy baseball? Baseball nuts, than whom there are no more fanatical fans in the universe. And they don't just shell out dough for baseballs. Arizona Diamondbacks' Luis Gonzalez sold a wad of bubble gum—*used* bubble gum—for ten thousand dollars. Somebody bought a set of Ty Cobb's false teeth for $7,475. And a besotted fan once forked over twenty-five thousand dollars for Nolan Ryan's jockstrap.

How much would you pay for a second-hand baseball bat? Somebody shelled out $1.26 million for the stick Babe Ruth used to swat his first home run in Yankee Stadium more than eight decades ago.

What, aside from their history, sets these bats, balls and jockstraps apart from all the other bats, balls and jockstraps in the locker room? Simple—they're signed.

The bat has "Babe Ruth" etched on it in large loopy letters. Ty Cobb's false teeth have his signature scrawled across the upper plate. And Nolan Ryan's jockstrap? Well—it's signed, okay?

Is this good for the players? You betcha. A name baseball player can pocket ten grand (tax-free, of course) just for sitting down and signing baseballs for a couple of hours of an afternoon. The great left fielder Ted Williams actually made more money signing autographs than he did in his whole career as a player.

But here's the ultimate irony for all those money-dripping, trivia-collecting maniacs out there—most of what they pay for is phony. The entire celebrity signature industry is awash in bogus autographs. Experts reckon that less than a quarter of all Marilyn Monroe and Elvis Presley signatures are legit. They say only 6 percent of signed Beatles memorabilia was ever touched by Beatle hands. Golfer Tiger Woods won't even sign his golf balls anymore because he's seen so many fakes out there.

As far as baseball memorabilia goes, the people who know say that 75 percent of the signed stuff on sale is inauthentic. Can't the fans figure this out? Can't they see a scam waiting to happen? You would think so. As former US federal prosecutor David Rosenbloom says, "Why is it that if someone gave you a

$50 dollar cheque signed by Derek Jeeter, you would call the bank, but if somebody charged you $900 for a signed jersey, you would say 'Thank you.'"

Even when the memorabilia is genuine, its value is illusory to say the least. Canadian comic book tycoon and megamillionaire Todd McFarlane once shelled out three million dollars (US) for the privilege of owning Mark McGwire's seventieth home run ball. A gobsmacking amount of moolah, but after all, no one in history had ever hit seventy home runs in a season, right?

Right—until the year after, when Barry Bonds came along and lofted seventy-three balls out over the bleachers in one season. McFarlane's ball went from being worth three million dollars to $7.99 with one swing of the bat.

Ah well. The long-suffering Chicago Cubs fans know how to treat a celebrity baseball. You remember the 2003 playoffs when Cubs fielder Moisés Alou leaped to snag a ball, only to have a fan in the stands snatch the ball out of his glove? Steve Bartman was the fan, and the ball that he caught became known as "the Bartman ball"—a voodoo curse that Cubs fans insist lost them the game and a chance to go on to the World Series.

Last month Cubs fans had their revenge. At Harry Caray's restaurant in Chicago, a chef served up the Bartman ball—which had been dissected and marinated in Budweiser for several months—in the form of a pasta sauce. Dedicated Cubs fans were able to dine on the object of their loathing and ultimately to . . . put it behind them, as it were.

Todd McFarlane, eat your heart out.

THE FOUNTAIN OF YOUTH: JUST AN ILLUSION?

> *I shall soon be six-and-twenty. Is there anything*
> *in the future that can possibly console us for not*
> *being always twenty-five?*
>
> —LORD BYRON

That Lord Byron—what a glutton. Devastatingly handsome, impossibly intelligent, a baron and a poet to boot. He was also a freelance warrior happy to battle on the front lines for revolutionaries in Italy and Greece when he wasn't Errol Flynning from lady's bedchamber to lady's bedchamber back in London. "Mad, bad and dangerous to know," Lady Caroline Lamb dubbed him—and what did he really want?

To be twenty-five years old. Grow up, m'lord.

There's no satisfying some people. David Copperfield is another case in point. (I'm talking about the magician, not the Dickens ragamuffin.) Here's a Jewish boy from New Jersey who starts off pulling rabbits out of hats and silk scarves out of sleeves and winds up as one of the most famous sleight-of-hand artistes on the planet, renowned for levitating Ferraris, floating over the Grand Canyon and making the Statue of Liberty disappear.

The man's made more television appearances than the CBC pizza logo. According to *Forbes Magazine*, Copperfield's raked in more than fifty million dollars annually for at least the past five years. You'd think he'd be satisfied to sit back in the hot tub with a mag of champers, occasionally wiping his brow with a royalty cheque.

But no. He has to go and discover the Fountain of Youth.

Claims he found it on Musha Cay—one of a cluster of tiny islands he owns in the southern Bahamas. Says it was easy to find. You just draw a line from Stonehenge in England to Easter Island off the coast of Chile; then draw another line from the pyramids of Giza to the pyramids of Mexico. The spot where the lines cross? There's your Fountain of Youth.

Actually, I just tried that with two hanks of butcher's cord and my grade eight illuminated Rand McNally globe. My strings crossed out in the middle of the Atlantic several thousand kilometres north and east of the Bahamas. But then I'm no magician.

The point is, Copperfield says he knows where the Fountain of Youth is and it just happens to be in his backyard. He knows it's for real because, he says, "You can take dead leaves, they come in contact with the water, they become full of life again . . . Bugs or insects that are near death, come in contact with the water, they'll fly away. It's an amazing thing, very, very, exciting."

I can . . . um, imagine.

Copperfield's not the first person to be bitten by the Fountain of Youth bug. The Spanish explorer Juan Ponce de León is famously supposed to have accidentally stumbled across Florida while looking for the fabled wellspring back in 1513.

Senor de León was a Juanny come lately in the find-the-fountain contest. Rumours and legends about fabulous healing waters have been bubbling up all over the civilized world since antiquity.

Not surprising really. It's the Byronic thing again—man's obsession with not only stopping the clock but winding it back has spawned an entire anti-aging industry. It's the reason wizened Orientals pay small fortunes for the opportunity to nibble powdered tiger penis and paté de rhinoceros horn. It's the identical impulse that sells Grecian Formula, buttock lifts and Botox injections. (Riddle: what do you call an aging television sportscaster who gets so many facial injections his mouth is frozen in a permanent rictus leer? A Botoxymoron.)

I digress. Back to David Copperfield and his amazing discovery—any chance it's true? Oh, absolutely—unless the Fountain of Youth is actually to be found in the lagoons of Chilca. Folks in that tiny Peruvian coastal village have a brisk little business going promoting the "miracle mud" of its healing waters, the therapeutic powers of which they insist come from UFOs passing overhead. Visitors can choose from the Lagoon of Miracles (acne, rheumatism, arthritis), the Lagoon of Enchantment (eyes, nerves, joints, low blood pressure) or the Lagoon of Mellicera (diabetes, bone ailments, low fertility).

Visa and MasterCard accepted.

Speaking of which, you can check out Mr. Copperfield's Bahamian retreat for yourself if you'd like. Visitors are welcome to visit Musha Cay. Accommodations are available for a mere $24,750. Per night.

Me? I'm pinning my longevity hopes on something much smaller than a Bahamian atoll. On a molecule, actually, called resveratrol. It's found in blueberries, cranberries, raspberries, mulberries and—O joy untrammelled—in the skin of red grapes, which is to say in red wine.

A Harvard Medical School study shows that in mice at least, resveratrol dramatically reduces age-related diseases like cancer, heart disease and Type 2 diabetes.

So let's review our options here: we can slather ourselves in Peruvian mud; drop twenty-five large (each) to dabble our trotters in Mr. Copperfield's backyard pond; or sit back in our chaise lounges with a couple of snifters and a litre of Okanagan red.

I know which one Lord Byron would choose.

AS ONE COOKIVORE TO ANOTHER

Man is the only animal that blushes. Or needs to.

That was Mark Twain's take on what separates humankind from the other critters that call Planet Earth home, but what really makes us different from all the other species?

Language? Heck no. I listen to robins and finches talking their beaks off every morning. And who knows what wolves are communicating in those long and haunting arias they sing after sunset?

Use of tools? No again. Chimpanzees use sticks to fish termites out of nests. Crows use rocks—and even parking lots—as anvils to smash open clams and mussels. My own dogs employ a simple tool to get out of the house and come back in whenever they please.

I'm it.

Some say humans are the only animals who create art. I say, check out the construction of a Baltimore oriole nest before you make that claim.

Is the fact that we're civilized what sets us apart from "lesser" beasts? Puh-leeze. Hitler? Mao? Pol Pot? Osama? The NHL? I rest my case.

Nope, according to an American professor by the name of Alfred Crosby, what separates you and me from lemurs, spider monkeys, *Australopithecus africanus* and neon-butted baboons is our ability to fry an egg.

More particularly, Crosby points out that *Homo sapiens* is the only species on the planet that takes the trouble to cook its food. He says that simple difference has made all the, er . . . difference.

Cooking food is a knack our Stone Age ancestors picked up about twenty-five thousand years ago. We'll never know exactly which Cro-Magnon or Neanderthal first accidentally dropped his raw deer haunch into the campfire, gingerly pulled it out, brushed off the ashes, took a bite and said, "Mmmm!" But we owe him plenty, says Professor Crosby. He argues that cooking allowed our forebears, for the first time, to do some of the work of digestion outside their bodies. It also transformed otherwise unpalatable or even inedible foods such as leathery meat and hard grains into relatively decent grub. A few million hot meals later, Stone Age man had evolved into a creature with a larger brain and a smaller gut.

Upgrading from carnivore to cookivore had an even bigger payoff—it forced humankind to get its act together. "Cooking, like hunting, obliged human hunters, gatherers, fire tenders and cooks to plan and co-operate," says Professor Crosby. "Chimps spend six hours a day chewing; cookivores spend only one."

I wish I could take pride in my mastery of this one unifying characteristic that separates us from the lesser orders, but the fact is—I can't.

I fricassee not. Neither do I barbecue, blanch, broil or griddle. Fact is, I don't cook. I'm not proud of it, but I'm also not sufficiently ashamed to sign up for a cooking course.

I am fortunate enough to share a home (and a dinner table) with one of the most sublime food-fixin' aficionadas in the nation, but if she went on strike I still wouldn't cook.

I'd just eat a lot of baloney sandwiches.

Or perhaps I'd win the lottery and spend the rest of my life treating my sweetie to three squares a day in five-star restaurants.

I'd be cool and sophisticated about it, though. Not like the American tourist I heard mouthing off in a Chinese restaurant last week. He was peering at the menu, reading out various dishes in a loud voice and guffawing over the strange and exotic names.

Then he came to bird's nest soup.

He waved for the waiter to come over and then bawled, "You tellin' me you serve actual bird's nests as food?"

The waiter said yes and explained that this particular bird used its saliva to cement the nest together.

"Whoa!" yelled the tourist. "Are you saying I'm supposed to eat spit from a bird? I'm not paying good money to eat something that comes out of a bird's mouth!"

The waiter asked if he would perhaps prefer to order something else from the menu.

"Yeah," said the tourist. "Just fix me an omelet."

GOT DEM OL' SMOKIN' BLUES

The newspaper reporter.

The image is thirty years out of date but it's iconic and endures. Look at him there—Johnny Deadline—in the busy newsroom, wearing that cheap, wrinkled suit with his loud tie askew, his snap-brim fedora pushed back from his forehead. He's crouched over his manual typewriter, pecking out his stop-the-press hot story with two fingers.

And but of course, a gasper hanging out of the corner of his mouth.

Gotta have the dangling cigarette.

A newspaper reporter without a cigarette is like Harry Potter without his specs. Snoopy without his doghouse. Ron MacLean without Don Cherry.

Yeah, well, forget all that. Employees of the Tribune company, a giant media conglomerate that owns a stable of American newspapers and television stations, have just learned that if they smoke, they'll be paying an extra hundred bucks a month over and above their regular medical insurance premiums.

A crusade against smoking reporters. Is nothing sacred?

'Tis but the latest assault on that sorry bunch of misfits in our midst, the tobacco-addicted. We've chased them out of bars and restaurants. We've banned their odiferous practice in our workspaces and government buildings. Ontario has passed a province-wide ban on smoking in all public institutions. Parts of California forbid smoking in parks and on beaches. How else can we put the boot in? Is there some new way we can make these wretches suffer even more?

Smokers fight back, but either their heart isn't in it, or thanks to the debilitating side effects of their habit, they just don't have the wind to put up a decent fight. Their latest pathetic sally is the smokeless smoke.

Really. Three Ontario entrepreneurs competed to buy the Canadian rights to a Chinese-made (oh swell! The folks who gave us lead-tainted kiddy toys) smokeless, tobacco-free cigarette.

How would a smokeless, tobacco-free cigarette work, you ask? Well, it involves a nicotine cartridge, a microchip and some water-vapour mist. Your smoker sucks on an imitation cigarette while a battery-driven microchip activates an atomizer that puffs out a nicotine-flavoured plume of water vapour.

Not quite as down-home friendly as lighting up a Marlboro, is it?

Such a change in such a short time. Is it really less than twenty years since smokers fired up with abandon on trains and buses, in waiting rooms and hospitals? Remember when airlines routinely reserved rows sixteen through eighteen for smokers?

Good luck to non-smoking passengers in rows fifteen and nineteen.

And offices. Nobody batted an eye if you lit up in the office. Hell, there was an ashtray on every desk. The air in a typical office was blue with tobacco smoke, both new and second-hand. Non-smokers were grievously outnumbered and suffered silently. When I worked in radio, even the studios held ashtrays and guests were routinely offered a cigarette "for their nerves."

How the worm has turned. It's a brave soul indeed who would flick his Zippo in an office setting these days. Firing up has become a firing offence at many firms in Canada and the US. Most office buildings are identifiable during office hours by the clots of desperate, shivering nicotine addicts clustered around their doorways, getting their fix.

Needless to say, one huge benefit for white-collar workers is that the air in their offices, once noxious and riddled with carcinogens, is now pristine and pure as a forest glen.

Not.

The latest news is that laser printers, fixtures in pretty well every office in the land, have been quietly spewing out particle emissions far deadlier than tobacco smoke since they were installed. In fact one study suggests that spending too much time near an office copier is worse than sitting by a guy puffing two packs a day in the next cubicle.

Ironically the office workers likely to be least affected by toxic printers are the smokers. They'll be out on the sidewalk having a smoke.

Is that a smoker's cough I hear—or is it smokers having the last laugh after all?

NOW FOR THE REAL NEWS

After nearly thirty years of banging out stories for dailies, weeklies and biweeklies, this is an embarrassing admission to make, but . . .

I've never understood newspapers.

The way they're laid out, I mean. The front page is usually full of stories about global warming, spiralling inflation, car bombings in Thehellandgoneistan or mass murders in Nebraska. Stories, in short, that have no bearing on my day-to-day life and upon which I have not the slightest influence.

It's not until I turn to page seventeen and spy the tiny "this just in" stories that the newspaper experience comes alive for me. You know the stories I mean. The five- or seven-centimetre filler stories that start off with headlines like Man Eats Airplane in Brazil.

Those are the stories that make reading the newspapers worthwhile. The ones that make your eyes bug out, your jaw drop and your brain go, Huh?

Such as? Such as the story that appeared deep inside an

edition of *The Times of London*. It told of a choir that assembled at Vauxhall Cross interchange, one of London's busiest and noisiest traffic intersections, and sang eighteenth-century folk songs at the traffic.

Huh? Or, put another way, why would a choir want to do that? Because 250 years ago the highway interchange was a popular public gathering place called Vauxhall Pleasure Gardens, and the music (by Thomas Arne) that they were singing had been performed there at that time.

I realize it's not exactly stop-the-press news, but the image of a dozen doughty British choristers serenading lorry drivers and cube-farm commuters intrigues me far more than a front-page account of Stephen Harper's latest press conference ever could.

Also from a British newspaper (*The Guardian*), a straight-faced report informs us that Sean Combs has decided to change his name—no, strike that—he's decided to "rebrand his commercial activities."

You see, Sean Combs isn't known by that name over there. In Britain Sean Combs is officially Diddy Combs. He used to be Puff Daddy Combs but he changed that to P. Diddy five years ago. Last year he changed it again to just plain Diddy, but that caused a problem with a London-based music producer Richard "Diddy" Dearlove, who sued P. Diddy-Diddy-Puff Daddy-Sean.

Whoever-he-is agreed to drop the Diddy, and the case was settled out of court.

Not sure what Mr. X is going to call himself next. I believe Diddley Squat is available.

And a story from the *Boulder County Business Report* tells the tale of Patrick Murphy, a Colorado environmental consultant with a thing about dog poop. Patrick is specifically concerned about dogs that leave their calling cards along a local hiking trail.

And he has evidence. Man, does he have evidence. By means

of a global positioning device, Patrick has documented and pinpointed precisely 1,492 mounds of dog poop on a one-mile (0.6-kilometre) section of the trail.

Patrick . . . have you considered stamp collecting?

But my all-time favourite Huh? story of the month has to be the saga of Scrappy the Dolphin and his wardrobe malfunction. Scrappy, a male bottlenose dolphin, is a regular denizen of Sarasota Bay in Florida. You could pick Scrappy out from all the other bottlenose dolphins right away.

Scrappy was the one wearing the black Speedo swimsuit.

Well, not wearing it so much as . . . stuck in it. Somehow Scrappy got the suit over his head and jammed against his pectoral fins. Officials at a marine mammal research institute feared that if the suit stayed on, it could have dug into his flesh deep enough to sever arteries. Solution? Take off Scrappy's Speedo, obviously.

Easier said than done. It took four hours, five speedboats and a total of thirty-one people to corner Scrappy, net him, cut the suit off and doctor his wounds.

Today Scrappy swims the waters of Sarasota Bay once more, nude and free.

Now that's what I call good news.

STUPID IS AS STUPID DOES

There is, as the cliché goes, good news and bad news on the human stupidity front, my friends. The bad news is that it appears we're actually getting stupider. The good news is that we may soon have an anti-stupidity pill to combat the condition.

Scientists at Germany's Max Planck Institute for Molecular Genetics claim to have synthesized the world's first nostrum to combat natural boneheadedness. Maybe. In clinical trials the German pill has definitely improved attentiveness and short-term memory.

But only in fruit flies and lab mice.

Still it's a start, and not a moment too soon, I say. Other scientific studies indicated that humankind's intelligence arc seems to be flattening out, if not cratering. This is new. Back in the 1970s a political scientist by the name of James Flynn became famous when he showed that scores on IQ tests were rising year after year—an average of three points per decade. By the mid-1990s that was no longer true. Professor Flynn is still around—he's professor emeritus at the University of Otago in

New Zealand—and he thinks he has an explanation. He attributes the rising IQ scores of the 1970s and 1980s to the trend to smaller families. This meant, the professor says, parents had more time to interact with each child. Now he thinks perhaps we've reached our saturation point.

"You can't really get the family much smaller than one or two kids," he says, "and eventually people do want to relax."

Oh, we're relaxing, all right—especially our stupidity standards. Consider the tale out of New York, where Kelly Coakley, a twenty-three-year-old office worker, is suing Starbucks for refusing to honour a coupon for one free, large, iced coffee. Starbucks says it was a mistake, that the special coupon was intended for a select handful of employees, but somehow ended up disseminated on the internet. Kelly says too bad—she wants compensation for her "suffering"—to the tune of US$114 million.

"A very conservative figure," her sleazebag lawyer purrs, considering how "betrayed" his client feels.

It leaves me with just one question: whatever happened to *nous*?

A lovely term, *nous* (rhymes with mouse). It comes originally from Ancient Greek but it's used by Brits to describe what we call common sense. There's not a lot of it around these days, but I did find a couple of nuggets.

Exhibit A: Jamie Lee Curtis.

What are the chances that the child of two cinema megastars (Tony Curtis and Janet Leigh) would turn out to be anything more than a brain-dead, egocentric Hollywood brat obsessed with breast lifts, serial rock-star lovers and collecting diamonds the size of pit-run gravel?

Not Jamie Lee. According to a feature article in *More* magazine, Curtis has turned her back on plastic surgery and anorexic dieting. She is past the half-century mark and sees no reason why she shouldn't have a fifty-year-old body, complete with love handles and turkey neck. She wears her hair short because it's comfortable and she wears a man's watch because she doesn't like to squint to see what time it is.

And unlike so many Hollywood limo-liberals, she thinks for herself. "For years I hung out with really smart Lefty people," she says. "I was this Lefty girl. But you know what? I don't know where I stand on abortion. I don't believe the state has any right to decide what happens in a woman's body. But on the other hand my life has been immeasurably changed by being a mother to two adopted children. I wouldn't be a mother if someone had aborted them."

Oh dear. Someone who doesn't see a hot-button issue in black and white.

I found one more common sense hero. Robert Hughes is a transplanted Australian turned famous art critic. And he's nothing if not plain-spoken. Awhile back on a return trip to Australia, he was almost killed when a car full of thugs—all of them with criminal records and drug habits—rammed his car at high speed. When he recovered he denounced his assailants as "low-life scum."

The Australian media crucified him for it. They called him a snob and a bigot and told him to go back to America. Hughes's response? "I am, after all, a cultural critic, and my main job is to distinguish the good from the second-rate. I prefer the good to the bad, the articulate to the mumbling, the aesthetically developed to the merely primitive, and full to partial consciousness. I don't think stupid or ill-read people are as good to be with as wise and fully literate ones, consequently, most of the human race doesn't matter much to me, outside normal courtesy and the obligation to respect human rights. I see no reason to squirm around apologizing for this."

How insensitive! How outrageous! How elitist!

Not to mention refreshing.

DID YOU WANT FRIES WITH THAT?

onsider the humble hamburger. Seldom has a popular human food combination—one ground beef patty, one bun—been more basic. This is, of course, before the garnishes—slice of onion, tomato, dill, mustard, relish, ketchup, mayo, etc., etc.—which are what makes the humble hamburger so enduring.

And endure it has. The nucleus of the hamburger—a thin slab of ground beef seasoned with onions—is almost as old as our country, having emigrated from Hamburg, Germany, back in the 1870s. It was another thirty years before somebody had the notion to stick the patty between two slices of bread. By the turn of the twentieth century, the hamburger was a popular treat in much of North America. It made its official international debut at the 1904 World's Fair in St. Louis, Missouri.

That's one theory. The truth is, the hamburger's origins are lost in the mists of time. Naturally half a dozen towns and cities have jumped to declare their burg the birthplace of the burger. For obvious reasons Hamburg, Germany, believes that it deserves the honour. But the village of Hamburg, New York, makes the same claim. They say the hamburger was born at their Erie County Fair back in 1885. Villagers throw a Burgerfest each summer to celebrate. You'll never guess what they serve.

New Haven, Connecticut, has also made a leap at hamburger immortality, claiming that a local greasy spoon, Louis' Lunch, invented the hamburger as a snack for harried businessmen back in the early 1900s. They should get points for longevity at least—they're still churning out hamburgers at Louis', although you wouldn't recognize the product right off. The folks behind the counter at Louis' are hamburger purists. They serve your meat patty on toasted bread, not on a bun. And if you ask for ketchup or mustard you'll get your hand slapped. Only cheese, onion and tomato allowed.

But anyone researching hamburger supremacy has to give consideration to the town of Seymour, Wisconsin. The story goes that back in 1885, a local by the name of Charlie Nagreen was having trouble unloading fried meatballs at his restaurant, when inspiration struck. Charlie took his meat flipper, mashed a meatball flat as a hockey puck and slid it into a bun. "Try this," he told a customer. "I call it a hamburger." The rest of the world may not buy Charlie Nagreen as creator of the hamburger, but his townsfolk do. Seymour's chief tourist attraction is its Hamburger Hall of Fame. There you'll find what may be the world's largest hamburger. It weighs in at about half a tonne.

Did you want fries with that?

It hasn't always been a smooth ride for the hamburger. Back in the days of World War I, when North Americans were none too fond of all things Germanic, a lot of patriotic rebranding went on. The town of Berlin, Ontario, became Kitchener.

And the hamburger became the Salisbury steak.

But by the end of the war, North America's favourite fast-food snack had its original name back, and it stuck—so much so that it spawned a host of imitators. The cheeseburger made its entrance in the early 1920s, followed by beefburgers, baconburgers, fishburgers, steakburgers, porkburgers and chickenburgers. Then fast food fry-boys really got inventive. In the 1940s turtleburgers appeared in Florida, followed by oysterburgers, oceanburgers, octoburgers and, umm . . . gatorburgers.

There are other burger mutants. Lobsterburgers and crabburgers of course. Not to mention buffaloburgers, rabbitburgers, goose-, duck- and even spamburgers.

The only Canadian nominee to Burgerdom's Hall of Fame that I could find was mooseburgers. I had one in Kenora, Ontario, about ten years ago. Dee-lish.

The most grotesque riff on the humble hamburger? I nominate Burger King's Double Whopper with Cheese. Downing one of these monsters is the caloric equivalent of eating five chocolate bars or ten fried eggs or chugalugging five pints of beer. Nutritionists reckon you'd have to walk a brisk fifteen kilometres to burn one off.

Most inventive hamburger offshoot? Well, there's a restaurant in my home town that sells a burger bun filled with choice lamb. A Lamburghini, of course. Almost as clever as the name of a chickenburger that's sold in a pub near Glastonbury Abbey— Knights of the Round Table country—in southern England.

Naturally the treat appears on the menu as Chicken Excaliburger.

I'm sure King Arthur would have approved. Roundly.

YOUR CALL IS IMPORTANT—NOT

One of the very few features I begrudgingly admire about fundamentalist Islam is the capacity to announce life-and-death fatwas. Imagine having the power to instantly outlaw any earthly annoyance that bugs you. Goodbye, all TV ads for United Furniture Warehouse. So long, elevator music, argyle socks and Starbucks nomenclature ("Will that be a Tall, a Grande or a Venti?").

And people! If I was made imam for a day, I'd be dishing out personal fatwas like Halloween candy. Adios, Paris Hilton. Aloha, Donald Trump. Adieu, Bloc Québécois.

Ah, but if I only had one fatwa to dispense, I know who I'd lay it on.

The SOB who invented the corporate phone tree.

You know phone trees? Of course you do. It's that technological hell you're transferred to whenever you dial up a government number. Or The Bay or the hospital or your phone company or . . . well, pretty much any commercial concern nowadays. It didn't take merchandising bean-counters long to figure out that they could save a bundle by firing their receptionists and replacing them with a tape recording of some honey-voiced automaton enunciating your options.

So what if it makes the ticked-off customer even more ticked-off? We're talking bottom line here.

"For sales and service, press one; for administration, press two; for accounts receivable . . ."

How about voice-to-voice contact with a living, breathing, human, pal? You got an option button for that?

Used to be you could leapfrog the prerecorded jungle by dialing zero and talking to the operator, but many companies have eliminated that escape hatch altogether.

Corporate phone systems would perhaps be just bearable if they weren't so sick-makingly hypocritical. The recorded voice usually launches the spiel by silkily murmuring, "Your call is important to us . . ."

Excuse me? Hold it right there. No. Wrong. What you are demonstrating is how exceedingly *unimportant* our calls are to you. If you cared about our calls (we used to call it customer service) you would lend a sympathetic ear attached to a knowledgeable human employee who could actually help us with our problems.

Instead you give us a metaphorical boot in the arse with a recorded message.

Bruce Cran, president of the Consumers' Association of Canada, doesn't think that's an accident. "Corporate phone systems are actually designed to aggravate you into submission," he told a *Globe and Mail* reporter recently. He says that fewer than one in a hundred unsatisfied customers will follow up a phone call with a letter of complaint.

That may be true, but it doesn't apply to Pat Dori of Hackensack, New Jersey. A few years ago Mr. Dori purchased a laptop computer from Dell Inc. He had some trouble with it and returned it to the company. Dell sent him back a second-hand machine with an inferior warranty. Pat Dori picked up the phone to complain.

And was engulfed in the first circle of corporate phone tree hell.

Every time he called, the Dell robotess would put him on hold, sometimes for half an hour. Each time he redialed, he would have to start again from square one. ("Well, you see I have this computer I bought from your company . . ..")

Pat Dori sat with the receiver to his ear in Hackensack, listening to a tape loop reminding him of how important his call was to Dell and getting madder and madder.

And then he had an epiphany. He remembered seeing a Dell kiosk at a local mall. The thought that swam into his brain was: if they have kiosks, you can sue them.

And he did. He had his lawyer serve the papers to a bewildered sales rep at the local kiosk rather than to Dell headquarters in Texas. Nobody from Dell showed up at the court case to represent the company, so the judge awarded Dori three thousand dollars. That got Dell's attention, because Dori now had the right to seize the assets of the local kiosk. A fleet of corporation lawyers descended on Hackensack to appeal the ruling, but by then the story had hit the papers. Dori was a hero; Dell Inc. was the baddie. The company settled with Dori quickly and quietly.

Sweet. I can only hope that when the Dell lawyers called Pat Dori to negotiate, he had the wit to answer, "Welcome to Pat Dori's phone tree. We're not in right now, but your call is important to us . . ."

NOGGINS ON TOBOGGANS

What do Canadians need? Sandra Racco, a city councillor in Vaughan, Ontario, knows what we need. Another law. A law that makes it obligatory for each and everyone of us, boy or girl, geezer or toddler, to wear a helmet while riding a toboggan.

Four words occur off the top of my head:

Give

me

a

break.

I would dismiss Councillor Racco's suggestion as the desperate plea of a politician in search of headlines on a slow news day if it wasn't for the fact that she's getting a lot of support for her idea. Other politicians are stroking their chins and climbing aboard what looks like a no-brainer vote-getting bandwagon. Doctors are being solicited by reporters to opine on air that, yes, by gum, toboggans do go fast and occasionally run into stationary objects like trees and rocks. Health Canada has even been nudged into recommending that all children wear helmets while sledding.

A doctor at the University of Alberta goes one better. He told an enquiring Sun Media reporter that head protection is advisable for "anything faster than walking."

Really, doctor? Does that include ballroom dancing? Badminton? Swimming laps at the community pool? How about sack races at the Sunday school picnic?

I suppose you could argue that, yes, if we strapped our kids into helmets as soon as they rolled out of bed in the morning, there would be a measurable decline in head injuries to minors, but where are we going with this? And where will it end? Why not just duct tape our kids in bubble wrap and lock them in the attic? Then they'd be really safe.

I don't know if it's fallout from 9/11 or mere media-induced hysteria, but there's an unnatural obsession with perceived danger out there of late. Last week I overheard a mother berating her preschooler in a mall for making eye-contact with a passerby. "What did I tell you, Johnnie! Don't talk to strangers! Stranger, danger!"

Not necessarily. A stranger might just be someone you haven't met yet. Like, say, the Dalai Lama.

We're cocooning our kids. We give them video games and cellphones and iPods, all of which insulate them from the real world and keep them tethered close by. Does any parent ever say "Run outside and play" anymore? Probably not. Stranger, danger.

We're not doing the kids any favours. It is possible to hide from life, but there's a price to pay. For instance, who do you think suffers more from asthma and allergies, North American or Third World children?

It's our kids. Scientists have found that the immune systems of North American kids are "unsophisticated." In our sterile homes and germ-free schools, they don't get exposed to enough microscopic intruders to be able to differentiate between real threats such as germs and benign foreign particles like dust particles, pollen and cat hair.

So when our kids' squeaky-clean immune systems detect any suspicious invader, they immediately go on red alert, triggering a rush of often bogus allergy symptoms.

The noggins on toboggans controversy is something like that. The worriers point out that across Canada, seven kids have been killed on toboggans in the past four years. What they don't mention is that that's seven fatalities out of several hundred million toboggan rides other Canadian kids took without incident. They also don't mention that three of those children were hit by cars driving past the bottom of the toboggan runs.

No helmet will save anyone from a tonne and a half of rolling metal and rubber.

So what are the odds of sustaining a brain injury while tobogganing? Andrew Coyne, a *National Post* columnist, crunched the numbers for sledding and tobogganing mishaps in Canada. He concluded that if you took eight rides each winter not wearing a helmet, the odds are you could toboggan safely for the next 125,000 years without mortally cracking your skull.

Moral of the tale: put a helmet on your tobogganing kid if it makes you feel better, but acknowledge that the motivation is your neurosis, not your child's perceived predicament—and let's leave the government out of the act. They've got enough to screw up without getting into toboggan legislation.

And remember, to keep oneself safe does not mean to bury oneself.

I didn't make that up. Seneca said it about two thousand years ago.

Seneca wouldn't know a toboggan from a toga, but he knew something about common sense.

FROM YOUR ROVING ROBOREPORTER

Half the jobs I've held in my life don't exist anymore. When I was a kid I spent a few summers stooking hay on my brother-in-law's farm. It meant trudging through a field, pitchforking sheaves of new-mown hay into teepee-like stacks to dry in the sun. Nowadays farmers use big, smelly combine-balers that vacuum the hay up from the field, bind it in tight, snug bales and spit it out in a tenth of the time.

I also worked years ago as a plumber's gofer, humping heavy cast-iron pipe from truck to job site. That job's gone. Cast-iron pipe is history, replaced by light-weight plastic.

And do ocean-going vessels even *employ* lookouts anymore? As a deck cadet on an oil tanker back in the 1960s, I spent many a lonely four-hour stint on late-night watch, standing on the bridge peering with red-rimmed eyes out into the darkness, looking for lights or the hulk of anything adrift that might do us harm.

Radar takes care of that chore nowadays.

I'm not complaining. Those were jobs best left to mechanical devices with nothing better to do. Still it's humbling to realize that you can be replaced by an assemblage of nuts and bolts hooked up to an engine. Remember the folk song about that nineteenth century steel-drivin' man, John Henry? He was, so legend has it, the strongest, fastest man ever to swing a sledge hammer. One fateful day he faced off against a steam-engine spike driver to see whether man or machine was better at laying railroad track.

John Henry won—sort of.

> Died with a hammer in his hand, poor boy
> Died with a hammer in his hand.

Ah well. It wasn't too much later in my life that I laid down my pitchforks and binoculars in favour of a typewriter and became a newspaper guy. After all, it would be a rainy day in Osoyoos before any machine could replace a reporter, right?

Not right.

Thomson Financial—an American news service that supplies market info to newspapers, television and radio stations across North America—has just introduced its latest crack team of news-writing staff members.

It's a bank of computers.

The machines have been programmed to intercept, interpret, write and transmit automated articles on stock market news. They can scan developments on, say, a corporation's earnings report, interpret the data with reference to current conditions and previous history and publish an actual news story on the event—within 0.3 seconds.

A Thomson spokesman said it's not about replacing reporters. It's "about delivering information to customers so they can make an immediate trading decision."

Sure. That's what the railway barons told John Henry.

Come to think of it, I once knew the newspaper equivalent of John Henry. His name was Jiggs O'Brian, and he was one of my early mentors in journalism. Jiggs was riding a copy desk at a struggling biweekly newspaper when I met him, winding up a downwardly spiralling forty-year career. Jiggs had seen it all and written about most of it, big and small, from coronations to long-lost-brother-reunion stories, wedding-ring-in-a-lake-trout stories and kitten-up-a-tree stories.

Was Jiggs jaded and cynical? No. Ozzie Osborne is jaded and cynical. Jiggs was . . . something else. I remember how he handled fire stories. Most reporters would relish the chance to chase a clanging fire engine and write an I-was-there story. Not Jiggs. He had special forms he kept in the bottom left-hand drawer of his desk, right behind the twenty-sixer of Captain Morgan. When someone phoned in a fire report, Jiggs would take one of the forms, roll it into his typewriter and start pecking in the blanks. The form went something like:

> City firemen were called out to deal with a ___ alarm fire that broke out at __a.m./p.m. yesterday/this morning/afternoon in the _____ district of the North/South/East/West ward. Fire Chief/Deputy Fire Chief/Acting Fire Chief _____ said there were __ casualties. Damage was estimated to be negligible/substantial/about $_____. Cause of the fire was faulty wiring/careless smoking/lightning/unknown/suspicious.

Good old Jiggs—just slightly ahead of Thomson Financial.

I should have seen it coming, of course. When I started out in the newspaper biz, any reporter worth his byline could write fluent shorthand. Hand-held tape recorders came along and took care of that. And for at least the past twenty years, my battered Olivetti has been relegated to duty as a spider incubation unit on the back shelf of my closet, replaced by my laptop computer. Gone are the days of carbon copies and messy, illegible copy paper. Nowadays, thanks to technology, I can hand in spotless, perfectly spell-checked copy that is literate, rational and #@&**^%$)**$!!^^#.|>?%%#*^@!&&+

ARTHUR IN LIMBOLAND

FAME: THE DARK SIDE

So I deliver this after dinner speech at a teachers' convention in Winnipeg, and it goes very well. They all laugh in mostly the right places and applaud warmly when I'm done. Nobody throws buns or offers to ride me out of town on a rail. After my speech a pleasant-looking woman approaches and says, "Hello, I'm [name withheld] from Kenora. I know how you feel about my town, but that's okay—no hard feelings."

Huh?

I've been to Kenora, Ontario, a few times. I like it well enough, but have no overpowering feelings about the place. Nothing spectacular—good or bad—ever happened to me in Kenora. So I ask the woman what she means.

"Don't apologize," she says. "I know that you used to work at the Royal Bank in Kenora. I know you wrote about the town and called it a hellhole, but that's okay."

Double huh?

I have never worked in Kenora. I have never worked in a

bank. But the more I try to convince the woman the huffier she gets.

"There's no point in lying about it," she tells me. "Everybody knows what you wrote."

Except I didn't. As I said, I don't have any history with Kenora and anyway I wouldn't be stupid enough to publicly diss a town where I might find myself looking for a motel room some evening.

Doesn't matter. Nameless lady—and who knows how many other Kenoraites—is totally convinced I gave the town a poison-pen review.

Ah well. I'm strictly a guppy in the celebrity fish bowl, but I've come up against the dark side of being known more than once. People phoning me up at 11:30 at night wanting to know the name of that wacky woman I interviewed on the morning show. Drunks buttonholing me in a restaurant to ask me if I can put them in touch with Don Cherry. Happens to me maybe once a month.

I can't imagine what life must be like for megacelebrities like Margaret Atwood or Leonard Cohen.

Or Robin Williams.

Actually, I don't have to imagine what the kooky side of stardom is like for Robin Williams—he laid it out to a reporter in Beverly Hills not long ago. He told of being accosted at a press conference by a woman he'd never met.

"Do you remember me?" she asked.

"No," said Williams truthfully.

"We met in Oklahoma," said the woman.

"Really?" said Williams.

"I worked for you for six months," said the woman.

"No, you didn't," said Williams. "I know who's worked for me, and there haven't been that many. Only two or three."

"Yes I did!" the woman insisted. As security people moved

in to escort the lady away, Williams recalls her yelling, "It was platonic!"

We think celebrities lead magical lives of privilege and splendour. Freebie wardrobes. The best seats in the best eateries. Laid-on limos. Wall-to-wall adoration.

But there's a price. Kenneth Tynan, the English critic, wrote of an incident in a London restaurant years ago. He was having dinner with the actor Richard Burton when a fan approached their table. His name was Walter, the fan explained. He was dining with some lads from his brokerage firm. It would mean so much to him and his career if Mr. Burton would just come over to the table and say something like "Walter! How good to see you!" Wearily Burton agreed to do it. A few minutes later he dutifully approached Walter's table and delivered his greetings. Walter looked up and drawled, "You again, Burton! For God's sake stop being a bore and leave me alone!"

Uproarious laughs from the table of stockbrokers. Tynan wrote of the indescribable look of sadness in Richard Burton's eyes.

Fame is not all roses and champagne. Dini Petty, a media star who made her name riding in a pink helicopter delivering traffic reports, told a magazine writer, "I think if I had to do it all over again I'd rather just be rich. I don't think that fame is worth a tinker's dam. It's very intrusive and the more you have the more intrusive it is."

Singer-songwriter Jane Siberry said it best. She sang, "I'd probably be famous now if I wasn't such a great waitress."

Of course that was before she became a celebrity.

SAVOIR FAIRE?
IT'S IN THE BAG, MAN

Way back when I was a lusty boomer in my twenties, I suddenly developed a crippling backache. I stood it for about a week, then I shuffled off to see old Doc Atkins, the only chiropractor in town.

"It's my lower back, Doc," I told him. "It's fine when I get up in the morning, but by evening it's killing me. And all I do is sit at a desk all day."

Doc Atkins was old school. He didn't have me fill out a medical history questionnaire. He didn't examine, diagnose or prescribe or put me up on the table for an adjustment. He just asked me a simple question: "Where do you carry your wallet?"

"My hip pocket. Why?"

"Put it in your front pocket."

That was it. Doc Atkins cured my backache with six words. Best twenty-five bucks I ever spent.

My backache disappeared, but it was replaced by a

headache—where to carry my wallet. It felt uncomfortable in my front pocket and made me walk like Chester on *Gunsmoke*.

So I graduated to a fanny pack, one of those pouchy things you sling around your waist. But that didn't work either. It made me feel too much like a tourist from Buffalo. Or a kangaroo from the outback. You can't wear a fanny pack with a suit or a sports jacket, and if you zip up your windbreaker over it, you look like you're smuggling drugs.

Besides, have you ever tried to get behind the wheel wearing a fanny pack?

I thought my troubles were over when I discovered the Tilley vest. What a find! Your average Tilley vest is built to withstand a nuclear attack and boasts more pockets than a billiard academy. It has inside pockets, outside pockets and pockets inside the pockets. Great! Finally sufficient storage to carry my reading glasses. And my notebook. Room for my Walkman. And my address book. Plus a couple of pens. Don't forget the car keys. And a pair of sunglasses. Even my harmonica! Still lots of space for that Robert B. Parker paperback I'm reading.

Oh, yes . . . and my wallet.

Well, you see the problem. I don't carry cigarettes, a lighter, a cellphone or a BlackBerry, but if I did, they'd be in there too. The Tilley vest solves my storage concerns, but thanks to my packrat nature, it adds about seventeen kilograms to my body weight.

And it makes me look like the Michelin Man.

Plus there are so many pockets it takes me an average of seven minutes to find anything in it.

I know full well what the real solution to my problem is, of course. I'm just having a little trouble accepting it.

I need a purse.

That's right—a sack, a grip, a ditty bag, a tote, a holdall. Something I can fill with my daily necessities and jauntily sling over my shoulder.

And why not? Why should women be the only gender that gets to haul half their life around in a handbag while we men are reduced to stuffing our pockets like squirrels or carrying dorky briefcases that make us look like cube-farm nerds?

We all know why not—it's because it's called a purse. My *Canadian Oxford Dictionary* defines purse as "a small women's bag of leather or fabric, etc., for holding small, personal articles . . ."

Women's bag. Men don't carry purses.

So the name's the only problem? Great. Let's change it.

Let's call it a murse.

Down with handbags—we'll have manbags. They don't have to be frilly or poncey—didn't Harrison Ford carry an over-the-shoulder canvas bag in *Indiana Jones*? That's virile enough for me.

So be warned: next time you see me you're going to marvel at my sudden, dramatic weight loss—about seventeen kilograms—and my newly svelte silhouette.

And if I detect even the hint of a smirk at what's slung over my shoulder, I'll smack you with my murse.

ARTHUR IN LIMBOLAND

One of the distressing byproducts of writing books for a living is that you get shanghaied into going on book tours.

Sounds glamorous: gallivanting across the country, free room, board and airfare, allowing rapturous fans to prostrate themselves before you and kiss the hem of your Tilley travel trousers.

Doesn't usually work out that way. This latest book tour took me to a lot of bookstores in Toronto, Ottawa, London, Windsor and oddly—little I knew just how oddly—Sarnia.

It went pretty well. Nobody heckled or threw tomatoes. Many even bought books.

Then the wheels fell off. Somewhere between Toronto's Pearson and Sarnia's Chris Hadfield airports, my trusty driver's licence fluttered unnoticed from behind my boarding pass and disappeared forever. I'd had it out, of course, as photo ID, which you have to show to get on airplanes these days. I reported the loss to Air Canada's lost and found desk and went on to appear at the Sarnia library to read from my latest book.

The next morning I plopped my bags in front of the Air Canada ticket counter, ready to board my flight home.

"Photo ID, sir?" said the attendant.

I explained how I had lost my driver's licence en route to Sarnia the previous evening and reported it—to this very counter, in fact.

"Photo ID, sir?" repeated the attendant.

Well no. But I did have my Visa, MasterCard, health care, Air Miles, CAA, Co-op membership, Royal Canadian Legion, library, ACTRA—even, dammit, my own Air Canada Aeroplan—card.

"Anything with your photograph on it, sir?"

Umm . . . my Costco card? Uh-uh.

I even had copies of my two latest books featuring my name in capital letters and my mug in full colour plastered across the front cover.

"Sorry, sir. Not acceptable."

One wants to scream out for a reality check. One wants to ask how much trouble Air Canada's vigilant minions think a Taliban fanatic would take to infiltrate the steely perimeter of Sarnia, Ontario, in order to—I don't know—blow up a Tim Hortons?

But one doesn't. One opts instead for a frantic fifty-dollar round-trip taxi ride to the local cop shop, hoping the Ontario Provincial Police will check one out and certify one as an unlikely Islamofascist agent in time to still catch one's flight. The cop on duty shrugs. "You'll have to wait until Monday and see a justice of the peace," he says.

Monday? It's Saturday morning!

Back to Sarnia Airport, an airport that lacks so much as a coffee vending machine. I use the one and only pay phone to call my partner on the other side of the country. She faxes copies of my passport, my social insurance card and my birth certificate to the airport fax machine.

The faxed copies "aren't clear enough." My partner, still on the other side of the country, drives into town to a photocopying store and repeats the procedure. This time the copies are "adequate." I am finally allowed to board a flight out of Sarnia and wend my way home about twelve hours later than planned.

Bitter? Who's bitter? Besides, look at it from airport security's point of view. There they are in Sarnia, Ontario, third only to Kabul and Baghdad as a hotbed of insurrectionist turmoil, confronting a pudgy, bald, Caucasian geezer with barely over a dozen pieces of identification.

Classic suicide bomber profile.

It would be hilarious if it wasn't all so damned stupid.

It would be excusable if it wasn't such a massive waste of everyone's time and energy and money.

Because this is a dreary one-act play repeated in endless, mundane variations at airports large and small right across the world these days. Octogenarian grannies being forced to remove their shoes. Half-spent tubes of Colgate being assiduously quarantined. Retired farmers from Estevan being disarmed of their nose hair tweezers.

And God help you if you check in with a suntan, no ID and a name like Abdul.

If Osama bin Laden is still alive, I know exactly how he's going to die.

Laughing his bony ass off.

LOOK ME UP WHEN URiNETOWN

For today's topic I have chosen urinals, subsection men's.

I appreciate that some readers may accuse me of setting the bar a little too low with this choice. To such readers I respond with a "pish!" Do such readers realize that our civilization has progressed to the point where it is now possible for a man to pee into a ten-thousand-dollar porcelain urinal sculpted as a jack-in-the-pulpit flower? Do they understand that *Fountain,* a sculpture by Marcel Duchamp, is the most important work of art of our time?

Well, not a sculpture so much as a plain ordinary urinal, previously ripped from some bathroom wall and submitted by Duchamp to the Society of Independent Artists exhibition at the Grand Central Palace in New York back in 1917. The exhibit was deemed indecent by the judges and turned down. Eighty-seven years later, in December 2004, five hundred of the most influential people in the British art world proclaimed *Fountain* to be the most significant piece of art produced in the twentieth century.

Yes, folks. We're talking about a urinal.

As for the ten-grand jack-in-the-pulpit *pissoir,* you'll find that beauty among the collected works of Clark Sorensen, a San Francisco artist who has also created one-of-a-kind urinals modelled on the pitcher plant, the calla lily and the California poppy as well as red and orange hibiscus.

And they truly are beautiful works of art. Check them out for yourself at www.urinal.net/naturescall.

They're stunning. Seems a shame that their entire *raison d'être* is to be peed on.

But that is the earthly destiny of the lowly urinal. Not that the inundated devices can't score impressive victories within the harsh parameters of their mundane calling. This wacky old world can offer levitating urinals, women's urinals and even talking urinals.

Levitating urinals? British Columbia's capital city has 'em—or will have soon, if some city councillors get their way. The devices, called urilifts, are two-metre high stainless steel cylinders that rise hydraulically from under the pavement at dusk and remain in place until the first rays of dawn. Sort of like vampires.

Urilifts are designed to relieve the city of a burgeoning problem: boozed-up louts who find themselves with full bladders after the bars close and don't much care where they empty them. Urilifts are already doing duty in Europe, but it looks like Victoria may be the first place on this side of the Atlantic to give them a test drive.

Will urilifts be a success? There are no sure things in the world of urinal innovation. Take, for instance, women's urinals. They've been around since the 1950s, but they've never really taken off.

It's not hard to figure out why. Thanks to their anatomy, men don't have to get up close and personal with a urinal. (Restroom attendants say we don't get close enough.) Women, on the other hand . . . well, vive la différence and all that, but there is, shall we say, a design problem that so far has eluded both technical boffins and arbiters of style.

But when it comes to talking toilets—we're all over that. If those lager louts who make downtown Victoria a smelly and slippery minefield after last call each night were to find themselves magically relocated in downtown Rio Rancho, New Mexico, they'd be in for an experience they wouldn't soon forget.

The restrooms in Rio Rancho restaurants and bars are open later, for starters. And they're much friendlier. A boozy fella could mosey up to a Rio Rancho urinal, make the necessary adjustments and . . . that's when he would hear a sultry woman's voice saying, "Hey, big guy. Having a few drinks? Think you had one too many? Then it's time to call a cab or a sober friend for a ride home."

Yep, it's a talking urinal. Well, a talking urinal deodorant puck, to be precise. The New Mexico department of transportation has installed more than five hundred of them in urinals throughout the state in an effort to reduce drunken driving.

A state spokesman figures the washroom is the perfect place to get the message across. "(In a restroom) guys don't chitchat with other guys," he says. "It's all business."

He's got that right—concerning the chitchat, I mean. I remember the story about Winston Churchill entering the men's room of the British House of Commons only to find his political opponent, Clement Atlee, already engaged. Churchill marched to the opposite end of the bank of urinals and took up his stance. "Feeling standoffish today, are we, Winston?" asked Atlee.

"Indeed," replied Churchill. "Every time your party sees something substantial you try to nationalize it."

SEND OFF THE CLOWNS

I've always known there was something wrong with me but I didn't know there was a name for it. Well there is—it's coulrophobia. Your obedient correspondent is—or at least has been— a raving coulrophobic. And don't risk a hernia hauling down the Oxford English; it means clown hatred.

The guys that circuses routinely employ to provide comic relief always freaked me out as a kid way more than the lions, the pythons or the Bearded Lady of Borneo. To me clowns were not amusing and harmless. They looked like eerie alien bogeymen. I never understood how everybody else could laugh at them. I wanted them rounded up and shot.

I guess I'm no longer a true coulrophobic. As an adult, being in the presence of a professional clown just makes me edgy and creeps me out. A certified coulrophobic would suffer a panic attack, maybe even a breakdown.

Should that be surprising? We're talking about encounters with total strangers wearing ash-white faces, hideously exaggerated makeup, light-bulb noses, neon spaghetti fright wigs and shoes the size of skateboards.

Is it a coincidence that one of the minor ogres of the twentieth century, serial killer John Wayne Gacy, used to entertain the neighbourhood kiddies dressed up as a character he called Pogo the Clown?

Lon Chaney Sr.—a guy who spent a good part of his career scaring the beejeebers out of moviegoers—had little good to say about the clown profession.

"There is nothing funny about a clown in the moonlight," said Mr. Chaney. David Kaye would doubtless agree. "To a toddler, there's nothing funny about a clown—he's a monster," he says.

David Kaye should know. His working name is Silly Billy. He is, yup, a professional working clown who specializes in entertaining at children's parties in New York City.

But he's not your typical clown. No bulbous schnozz or Phyllis Diller cosmetics for Silly Billy. "I don't wear makeup or a fake nose," says Silly—er, Mr. Kaye. "My jumbo-sized glasses are the only thing that makes me a clown and not just a guy who is badly dressed."

Seems to work just fine. Silly Billy has lots of work and no reports of terrified audience members.

But coulrophobia is not an ailment that's restricted to the younger set, as promoters for a rock festival in Britain found out recently. Organizers of an event called Bestival had rented a venue on the Isle of Wight and were looking for a gimmick to sell tickets. "I know!" yelped one organizer. "Let's have a circus theme! Monkeys! Elephants! Lion tamers! And we'll give discounts to all ticket-holders who come dressed up in clown outfits!"

Bad concept.

The idea of listening to rock bands surrounded by a sea of strangers all dressed like Bozo was such a turn-off to so many people that the organizers had to abandon the idea and declare Bestival a clown-free zone.

Sadly some coulrophobics remain stricken even after they've swept clowns out of their life. Regina McCann is a twenty-eight-year-old New York state resident who works in a funeral home. She can handle that part of her life. What she has trouble with are the nightmares that visit her regularly. She dreams that she's in her car late at night driving down a deserted street, being pursued by "a whole bunch of clowns on stilts of different heights."

Sounds kind of goofy if you've never experienced coulrophobia. For those of us who have, it's not goofy at all, it's chilling.

Personally I've never had dreams in which I'm pursued by clowns, but if I ever do, I know how I'll respond.

When the clowns run me to ground and start to surround me, I'll be looking for one specific clown in the pack. And when I see him, he can expect no mercy. After all, I know a little Kung Fu.

Yessir. I'm gonna go straight for the juggler.

WE LIVE IN SENSITIVE TIMES

Men, be vigilant. There is an ominous danger aswirl in the Canadian ether that threatens to play Whac a Mole with your sense of self-worth and ultimately rip your manhood from your person to leave you whimpering wimpishly like a small-L soprano.

And its name is RONA.

I'm not talking about Rona Ambrose, the Tory bigwig with the gorgeous hair (as opposed to Stephen Harper, the Tory bigwig with the hair that looks like, well, a big wig).

I'm talking about RONA, the Montreal-based, Canada-wide home and garden hardware retail giant with 540 outlets and counting. RONA wants to sell you home and garden improvement stuff and its sales strategy is diabolical.

You may have seen the TV ad. It shows a (female) customer in a RONA store talking to a (female) clerk. She is complaining about her doofus, layabout, know-nothing (male) husband who, she says, is about as much help around the house as the dust bunnies under the marital bed.

"That's okay," says the (female) clerk. "They (the husbands) are all like that."

Personally I'm not offended. Maybe that's because I don't think it's a bad thing to laugh at ourselves from time to time. But most likely it's because I am that doofus, layabout, know-nothing husband incarnate. I am not a handy guy. My idea of a garden improvement is fluffing the pillow on the hammock. I am okay with that ad.

Peter Regan, on the other hand, is not. Mr. Regan is a forty-seven-year-old single parent who lives in Calgary. He took huge offence when he saw RONA's ad making mock of masculinity. "Why is it okay to bash men?" he asked.

Now there was a photograph of Mr. Regan in my morning newspaper. It showed him edging his garden and frowning meaningfully into the camera. Mr. Regan is exceedingly broad of shoulder and meaty of thigh. I'd guess he would run about 115, maybe 135 kilograms. He would not look out of place in the defensive line of the Calgary Stampeders. If I ever decided to bash a man, I wouldn't pick Peter Regan.

I'd have assumed that Mr. Regan would be robust enough to weather a thirty-second home and garden TV ad poking gentle fun at men's ineptness, but I'd have been wrong. Mr. Regan was hurt. And when a RONA spokesman told him that the ads were meant to be humorous, he got furious. "At what point do you stop joking around," he asked. "This portrayal of men as knuckle-dragging Neanderthals or habitual lazy drunkards robs our boys and families of role models."

Umm, Planet Earth to Peter Regan: life is not a Boy Scout commercial. Homer Simpson is a lousy role model too. So are the misfits on *King of the Hill* and *Beavis and Butt-Head*, but they make us laugh. That's all they're intended to do.

Is it just me, or are we all getting just a tad too hypersensitive these days?

Apparently it's just me, because Peter Regan complained

to Advertising Standards Canada—and they agreed with him. RONA has been ordered to either yank or amend the commercial so that it no longer "disparages men and/or married men."

Ho-hum. A restaurant down in Louisville, Colorado, has been ordered to change the name of its signature sandwich, something it's been advertising and selling for the past eighty-eight years. New name of the sandwich? The Italian burger. Name under which it has been sold for most of the past century? The Wopburger.

Well—no contest, right? Extremely offensive name to Italians.

Except for one thing: the Wopburger was created and named by Italian immigrants Michael and Emira Colacci—as a tribute to their Italian heritage. They had a sense of humour. The Colorado bureaucracy did not. Richard Colacci, owner of the Blue Parrot Diner and grandson of the pioneers, says, "Losing our Wopburger is hard to take."

Get used to it, Richard—it's going around. In fact it's not just going around, it's coming full circle. According to a news report in the *Melbourne Herald Sun* in Australia, there's a bar in town that has just been granted the right to refuse entry to any customer who is a practising . . . heterosexual.

It's a gay bar, you see. The owners of the bar maintain that allowing straight men and women onto their premises would "destroy the atmosphere which the company wishes to create."

Oh—and it's a male gay bar. So lesbians are excluded too.

Sometimes to get into an ordinary bar you have to show your driver's licence.

I don't want to guess what you have to show to get into that bar in Melbourne.

PEACE ON EARTH

Consider what you tell the world with the index and middle finger of one hand.

Pop those fingers up against your temple and you're telling everyone that you're a loyal member of Lord Baden Powell's own—you're a Boy Scout.

Hoist those fingers in a tavern and you've just ordered a couple of beers—if you catch the waiter's eye.

When posing for a group photograph you can hold the two fingers up behind someone's head just before the flashbulb pops. It's called giving someone bunny ears. It's also called being a dork.

And you can make wiggly V signs with both hands to form "air quotes" giving ironic distance to something you're saying. I'm sure Mark Antony was tempted to use V signs in his eulogy to Caesar when he said:

> Yet Brutus says that Caesar was ambitious
> And Brutus is an [air quote] honourable man [air quote].

Very handy, the V sign, but if you happen to employ it over-seas—particularly in England, Ireland or New Zealand—be sure your palm is facing outward not inward. Two fingers up (slightly curled) with knuckles facing outward means something quite, ah, different over there. It's the most insulting gesture you can make, but with a fascinating history. Legend has it that the bowfinger salute, as it's called, goes back about six centuries to the Hundred Years War between England and France.

One of England's deadliest weapons at that time was the longbow, which archers used with great accuracy from aston-ishing distances. The French feared the English longbowmen, and whenever they captured one, made a point of chopping off the archer's index and middle fingers—the ones used to steady the arrow on the bowstring—so that he could never again be a threat. Before battle, unmutilated longbowmen would waggle their two bow fingers defiantly at the French forces to indicate that they were in fine shape, and a blizzard of incoming English arrows could be expected imminently.

That's the legend, and if it isn't true it ought to be.

But that's the rude V sign. The more polite V sign (palm outward) was also championed by an Englishman of note. Sir Winston Churchill made it famous as a victory symbol during World War II. Many a Pathe newsreel would show the doughty, embattled PM trudging through the rubble left from yet another German bombing raid, then turning to face the cameras and hoisting a pugnacious V-for-victory salute, frequently with a fat cigar clenched in his bulldog jaw.

Speaking of embattled politicians, Richard Milhous Nixon appropriated the gesture as well, stealing it—as was his wont—from the burgeoning anti-Vietnam War peace movement in the 1960s. Once, when faced with a street-full of war protest-ers in California, Nixon flashed them the double V sign. The crowd raged; Nixon cackled. "That's what they hate to see," he sneered.

Nixon had his own ironic involvement with the famous symbol. His last gesture as president of the United States? A grotesque parody of the V sign as he hunched over just before boarding the helicopter that would whisk him away from Washington forever.

Just two fingers raised, the others clenched below, palm outward. Such a simple gesture, but what a long, strange history it's had. Today it's safe to say that the gesture signifies peace much more than victory, particularly as it's come to be identified with the world famous peace symbol, the one that looks like a trident inside a circle. That icon started off as the logo for the Campaign for Nuclear Disarmament but expanded to become the symbol for the peace movement in general.

Well, for most of us, but not for Bob Kearns. Mr. Kearns is the president of a homeowners' association in Pagosa Springs, Colorado. Recently he had to order Lisa Jensen, a resident of Pagosa Springs, to take down a Christmas wreath on her front porch.

Reason? The pine boughs of the wreath were configured in the shape of a peace symbol, and that, according to Bob Kearns, was just . . . satanic.

"The peace sign has a lot of negativity associated with it," said Kearns. "It's also an anti-Christ sign. That's how it started."

Once the press got hold of the story and made him the laughing stock of late-night television, Bob Kearns relented and decided the wreath could stay.

Comforting. And speaking of comfort, I want all my readers to know that the index and middle fingers of both my hands are extended—palm outward—to all of you. I wish you happiness, prosperity, and above all, peace.

And Bob Kearns, if you still find that gesture threatening or Communistic or the work of the devil, well . . .

You're welcome to make do with my middle finger.

YOU CAN'T ALWAYS BELIEVE
WHAT YOU SEE

They say a picture is worth a thousand words, but whoever said it was seriously low-balling the powers of the visual. A picture—as in a photograph—can be worth way more than that. Here's the story of three photographs: one turned the course of a war, another destroyed an industry and a third torpedoed the career of a would-be prime minister of Canada. What's more, the photographs were lies.

Or rather they misrepresented what they showed. Harry Callaghan, a famous American photographer, once said, "A photographer is able to capture a moment that people can't always see." Which is true, but it's also true that a photographer can sometimes produce a picture that completely misrepresents reality.

Consider one of the iconic photos on the twentieth century, the fiery explosion of the Zeppelin *Hindenburg* over Lakehurst, NJ, in 1937. The photo looks like something Goya might have painted. It shows showers of sparks and flames billowing out of the cigar-shaped craft as it drifts earthward like a stricken whale. The photo made the front pages of newspapers around the world.

It also killed the Zeppelin business stone dead. Before the *Hindenburg* crashed, Zeppelins were considered the safest and by far the most pleasant form of air travel around. Regular flights ran between Europe and the US. Passengers dined on white linen with real silver and listened to dance bands as their craft wafted back and forth over the Atlantic. There was talk that Zeppelins would soon replace luxury liners—even trains.

One photograph changed all that.

The irony? The *Hindenburg* disaster wasn't that big a deal. Only thirty-six of the ninety-seven passengers on board died. New Jersey's highways routinely claimed more lives on an average holiday weekend. The fact is, if there hadn't been photographers on the scene to record the horrific explosion, Zeppelins would probably be a commonplace sight in our skies today.

Flash forward to 1968. Again, one morning the front pages of newspapers around the globe carry a single, stark, horrifying photograph. It was taken on the streets of Saigon and shows a man in combat fatigues calmly putting a bullet into the head of a Vietnamese who is young, handcuffed and incongruously wearing a plaid, short-sleeved shirt.

The executioner looks like a callous murderer, and the photo generated knee-jerk revulsion and an instinctive backlash against the Vietnam War and the US role therein. Everybody felt instant empathy for the poor young man so summarily dispatched.

Again irony raises its gnarled head. The "poor young man" was captain of a Viet Cong terrorist squad that had slaughtered dozens of unarmed civilians that day. His executioner was the Saigon chief of police.

But that's not the story the photo told. From the moment the picture hit the papers, the police chief's life went into a downward spiral. He lost his job and emigrated to Australia, where he was shunned like a leper. He went to the US, where he ran a restaurant for awhile—until his identity was disclosed as "that killer in the photo" and he was driven out of business.

Eddie Adams, the Associated Press cameraman who took the photo, won a Pulitzer Prize for it, but it didn't give him much pleasure. As he later said, "The general killed the Viet Cong; I killed the general with my camera."

Doug Ball could relate to that. He was a photographer with Canadian Press back in 1974, assigned to Robert Stanfield's campaign to become Canada's nineteenth prime minister. On a cross-Canada swing, the campaign airplane landed in North Bay for refuelling. Everybody got out on the tarmac to stretch their legs. Someone produced a football to throw around. Stanfield was game. Doug Ball got out his camera.

He shot an entire roll—thirty-six exposures—of Stanfield playing catch. He ran into the terminal and had Air Canada Express send the film to CP headquarters in Toronto for possible inclusion in the next day's newspapers.

Most of the photos Ball took showed Stanfield either throwing or catching the football with surprising grace and elegance. Only one of the photos showed him knocked-kneed, hands grasping empty air and wincing as the ball squirted out of his grasp. Guess which photo the newspaper editors chose.

When the *Globe and Mail* came out the next morning, there was the photo splashed across the front page with the headline "A Political Fumble?" Southam News columnist Charles Lynch, who was also on the campaign plane, asked Doug Ball if he'd taken the picture that was on the front page of the *Globe*.

"When I said yes," Ball recalls, "Lynch said, 'Trudeau just won the election.'"

And he was right.

Eddie Adams, the Pulitzer Prize winning photojournalist, once said, "Still photographs are the most powerful weapon in the world."

He was right too.

SANTA İNSANİTY

Well, the year is winding down, fading to a microdot in history's rear view mirror, and not a moment too soon—particularly if you answer to the name Claus, S.

It was not a good year for the jolly gent from north of 60. Santa was fingered by the Thought Police and wound up slugged, mugged and everything but tasered into a ball of molten tinsel 'neath the Christmas tree.

First indication I had that Santa was in for trying times came in an email back in early December from my pal Roy. "Dear Arthur," it reads. "I just read a piece in the paper noting that certain politically correct organizations are changing Santa's classic cry to 'Ha, ha, ha!' The reason? They don't want to offend persons of Asian descent."

Actually, Roy, I think some sadistic fiend out there in cyberspace just dreams up this crap to make us all crazy. The variation I heard was that "Ho, ho, ho!" was being dropped because it was "offensive to women." Bluestockings felt that it sounded too much like a pimp taking a staff roll call.

That wasn't the only assault on Santa's sanctitude. The US Surgeon General badmouthed him too. Rear Admiral Steven K. Galson griped that Santa was setting a poor example for the nation's youth. Why? Too fat, too lazy, too addicted to junk food.

"It is really important that the people who kids look up to as role models are in good shape, eating well and getting exercise," the Surgeon General harrumphed.

Then there was the troubling question of Santa's—ahem—moral character. The US Postal Service required all volunteers answering Santa's thousands of letters last year to sign a waiver releasing the Post Office from all liability for lawsuits from disgruntled parents.

Pretty much the same story in England where Microsoft Corporation was forced to shut down a British Talk to Santa website after the chat 'twixt kiddies and the Head Elf turned a little blue. A Microsoft spokesman said the company's engineers tried to sanitize Santa's salty vocabulary, but finally just pulled the plug on the whole program.

Even we here in the Great White North joined in the slagging of Father Christmas. Moya Green, president of Canada Post, declared war on "inappropriate letters" exchanged between some volunteer Santas and a few of the Canadian tots who each Christmas write to Santa care of North Pole, Canada, H0H 0H0.

"We apologize to those families affected and are taking every step possible—including co-operating with the police—to find the people who did this and to ensure there are no repetitions," Ms. Green said.

Cindy Daoust, the director of the Santa mail program, told reporters, "We are now ensuring that we have a full record of the names of each letter-writer alongside the volunteer handling the response. We will keep a master list or signoff sheet that will allow us to track who is responsible for each letter."

O brave new letters-to-Santa world. And just how many of the million-plus Canadian children who write to Santa each year received tainted letters that Christmas? Canada Post has had exactly nine reports of families getting mail with inappropriate messages.

Nine out of a million. Not exactly a landslide of corruption and moral turpitude.

But one can't be too careful when it comes to portly strangers bearing gifts in these perilous times, particularly bearded strangers in outlandish suits. Strangers who laugh just a little too much. Frankly I'm surprised this guy wasn't busted years ago for running a sweatshop manned by vertically challenged migrants slaving in penal servitude.

And where the hell's the SPCA? Why aren't they slapping Santa silly with cruelty-to-animals charges? Eight wild reindeer lashed to an overladen sleigh and expected to haul it around the world in one triple-overtime night shift without so much as a coffee break? Jack Layton, are you reading this?

And if the Ministry of Transport ever gets wind of Santa barrelling through restricted air space in an unregistered UFO with no horn, no brakes, no running lights—without so much as a flight plan or even a licence plate—if they ever pull him over, Santa will wind up *making* licence plates from now until palm trees grow where his workshop used to be.

Or alternatively we could all just lighten up. I leave the last word to Julie Gale. She runs a worldwide campaign against child exploitation called Kids Free 2B Kids. Her take on the Santa kerfuffle?

"Gimme a break," says Gale. "We're talking about little kids. Leave Santa alone."

Amen and a hearty ho, ho, ho to that.

THiS CAB RiDE BROUGHT
TO YOU BY . . .

My pal Henry has a good question. How come, he wants to know, the only people smart enough to balance the budget, fix our health care system, win the Stanley Cup and bring about world peace are all driving taxis?

He's got a point. Some of the most spirited—if one-way—conversations I've ever sat through have taken place in taxis. They weren't conversations, really, more like monologues. You don't want to get disputatious with a guy who's careening through downtown traffic like Charlton Heston in *Ben Hur*, all the while tossing *bon mots* over his shoulder into the back seat.

I've had cab drivers who know for a fact that Elvis is alive, that the US government is hiding a flying saucer in New Mexico, that the World Trade Center towers were dynamited by Rosicrucians and the problems in the Middle East are all caused by unleavened bread. ("It's zinc. Them Arabs don't get no zinc in their diet. Give 'em white sliced bread—problem solved.")

Ah well. If Matthew Rothschild gets his way, we won't have

to worry about loquacious cabbies much longer. We won't be able to hear them over the commercials.

Rothschild is a twenty-four-year-old whiz kid from Victoria whose latest brainwave is video commercials in cabs. Here's how it will work. You'll hail a cab, climb into the back seat and give the driver your destination, and just before he takes off—flip, bam! Down comes a DVD video screen out of the ceiling where the dome light used to be.

Will the video screen offer baseball recaps, news bulletins, old *Sopranos* reruns? No. It will play advertisements and nothing but advertisements. Rothschild is currently flogging ad space in fifteen-, thirty-, and sixty-second clips—and it ain't cheap. A fifteen-second clip will set an advertiser back $750 a month. For a full minute the rate is $2,450 a month, and that's just for the time. Advertisers will also have to pick up the tab for getting the ads created and produced on DVD in the first place.

Right now Rothschild has six minutes of uninterrupted advertising lined up and ready to go, but he hopes to up that to fifteen minutes, because he reckons that's the length of the average taxi ride.

Gee, I guess if you took a longer ride or got stuck in traffic you'd get to see the ads all over again.

Is this idea going to fly? It already is. Rothschild, who is president of MegaMedia Advertisements Inc., has struck a deal with the Yellow Cab franchise in Victoria, BC. As of this writing, ninety Victoria Yellow Cabs are carrying DVD screens which, says Rothschild, drivers will be instructed to activate at the beginning of their shifts.

So I guess that means that the taxi drivers will get to hear the advertisements over and over again throughout their whole shifts. They must be beside themselves with excitement.

But you've got to hand it to Rothschild—he's tracked down and cornered perhaps the last captive audience available, the defenceless taxi passenger. We've grown used to being hit in the earhole and the eyeball with commercials in airplanes and shopping malls, in fast-food joints and hospital waiting rooms. They've even got video ads in elevators, for heaven's sake. It was only a matter of time until the sanctity of the taxicab was breached.

How did Matthew Rothschild come up with this umm, brainwave? He's been working on it for the past two years, but the light bulb came on for him about five years ago.

"I was in the back seat of a cab and thought there had to be something to make the ride more interesting," he says.

Actually there is, Matthew. They're called windows.

Call me a Luddite and a curmudgeon, but I don't think I'll be hailing any Yellow Cabs in Victoria anytime soon. I've got enough unsolicited commercials infesting my life.

On the other hand, if it's raining and a Yellow Cab's the only one around, I'll hail it.

And if the driver starts to try and tell me how the Maple Leafs could win the Stanley Cup—I'll ask him to turn on the video commercials.

UMMM, MAYBE LATER

Never put off until tomorrow what you can put off until the day after tomorrow.

—Mark Twain

So I'm sitting on my favourite stool in one of my favourite public establishments, sipping my favourite beverage (relax, Ma, it's coffee, and decaf at that) when a wild-haired guy looms up in front of me and says, "We need to talk."

"Why?" I say.

"Why not?" he says.

So we talk. Or rather he does. Turns out he thinks he's "a pretty funny guy" and wants to write a newspaper column. He wants to know how I got started. How much I get paid. But mostly, "How long does it take you to write one of those things anyway?"

Oh boy.

All right, let's consider the modest screed unspooling before your eyes, right now, dear reader. When you get to the end you will have read (I trust) seventy to seventy-five sentences, give or take. That's about 780-odd words. Approximately half a page of tabloid newspaper space, if the editor has been generous with his type size.

And how long did it take me to write those 785 words?

Seven days.

It always takes me seven days, because I have to write a new column every week, and I start on next week's column the moment I send this week's to the editor.

Sort of. Column writing is a delicate business. You can't just fire up the computer and rattle it off. It's like a Japanese tea ceremony; certain rituals and ancient customs must be observed. For instance, on the dawn of the first day of tackling a new column I find it helpful to smash my left fist down on the alarm clock and bag an extra hour or so of sleep. That way I can approach the new column refreshed and rested.

I also believe in writing discipline and decorum. I know some of my more slovenly colleagues happily slump in front of their monitors and peck out their prose dressed in rumpled pyjamas and three-day beard stubble. Not for me, thank you. I don't go near my desk until I've shaved, showered, etcetera'ed and picked out my wardrobe for the day. By then it's time for breakfast. No point in writing on an empty stomach, right?

No point in trying to kick-start a cold motor, either. I always take time after breakfast to do the cryptic crossword in my morning paper to get the creative juices flowing. Cryptics can be tough. Often the clues contain allusions to politics or sports. I find it helpful to digest the entire newspaper before I even try the crossword.

Usually I have the crossword finished by 10 a.m., about the time my dogs are clamouring for their morning walk. Other people go to the gym, swim lengths, lift weights; I walk the dogs. I don't try to hurry it or cram it into a twenty-minute time slot. Proper dog walking can pretty much eat up the rest of the morning. But they're worth it.

After lunch a post-prandial torpor takes hold, making the

eyelids heavy and any thought of intellectual work (i.e. column writing) highly unattractive. As a writing professional, I never give in to this feeling. Instead I resurrect the crossword and vigorously attack the remaining unsolved clues until sleep overtakes me.

My barking dogs invariably awaken me before the entire afternoon is lost. A perfect time to get up and get working on that column—except as the dogs so clearly indicate, it's time for their afternoon walk. By the time we get back to the house, the dinner gong is sounding. Hi-ho. What's a struggling writer to do?

Evenings are not very productive, I find. There are chores to take care of, phone calls to respond to, and besides, *The Simpsons* is usually on. I try to get to bed early because morning comes all too soon, and I have an alarm clock to bushwhack.

This is pretty much the pattern for the first six days of my writing week. On the seventh day I arise like a samurai warrior. Grim. Determined. I barely glance at the crossword. On this day my partner walks the dogs. I sit down at my desk, fire up the computer, poise my hands like incoming eagle talons over the keyboard and . . .

Notice how messy my desk is. I straighten things up. I check my email. I sharpen my pencils, check my email again, reset my computer clock, check the email to see if I've had any late deliveries, and then . . .

bitethebulletputmynosetothegrindstoneputmyshoulderto-thewheelrollupmysleeves

pullmyselfupbymybootstrapskeepmyeyeontheballand JUST WRITE THE DAMN COLUMN!

Let's see, that's . . . 777 . . . 778 . . . yep, 779 words.

There now. That wasn't so hard, was it?

ANYBODY SEEN A DINOSAUR?

*Museums, museums, museums. Object-lessons
rigged out to illustrate the unsound theories of
archeologists; crazy attempts to co-ordinate and get
into a fixed order that which has no fixed order
and will not be co-ordinated! It is sickening! Why
must all experience be systematized?*

—D.H. Lawrence

I see where Canada's most famous museum managed to mis-
place an entire twenty-five-metre-long dinosaur skeleton. For
nearly half a century.

Doesn't surprise me in the least.

Our most famous museum? Unquestionably the Royal
Ontario—known to millions, affectionately and otherwise, as
the ROM. It squats at the corner of Bloor Street and Avenue
Road—ground zero for the urban upper-crustians in the Centre
of the Known Universe. The ROM has occupied the same
space since the beginning of World War I. In the near-century
in between it's had more facelifts than Phyllis Diller—the latest one being a ludicrous cubistic encrustation grandly known
as Renaissance ROM. It's a sharp-angled agglomeration of

aluminum and glass that juts, ten storeys high, out and over the main entrance. It looks as if a gigantic mutant sugar crystal dropped from the heavens and lodged itself in the building like an ill-placed sliver.

But that's cosmetics. Inside, the grand old ROM really is grand—Canada's grandest and the fifth largest museum on the continent. It is home to forty galleries and more than six million items, from Egyptian mummies to Algonquin amulets.

And not forgetting the dusty skeleton of a twenty-five-metre *Barosaurus* dinosaur that the Museum "discovered" in the basement last November. Apparently the museum acquired the skeleton back in 1962, put it in storage and then forgot about it altogether.

Why am I not surprised? Because for one summer, as a teenager, I worked at the Royal Ontario Museum—back about 1962, as a matter of fact. And from what I saw, losing a dinosaur skeleton the length of two subway cars would be a walk in Queen's Park for the ROM. Understand that I was not employed as a paleontologist, archeologist, curator, exhibit technician or anything grand like that. I was a lowly roofer's apprentice brought in to handle the grunt work while my more skilled colleagues replaced some air ducts and reshingled part of the roof.

This is supremely boring work on most buildings, involving as it does crawling through dusty, cobwebbed attics festooned with forgotten junk, bats, rats and occasionally unidentifiable and odiferous blobs of dubious biological provenance.

That's the way it is in most attics, but at the ROM—hoo, boy.

The first thing I saw when I pushed back the attic hatch was a welter of arcane weaponry that could only bring joy untrammelled to the heart of any teenaged boy. There were Prussian lances and Indian tomahawks, Spanish swords and Italian stilettos. There were bows and arrows, a blunderbuss, several ancient long guns and the strangest "weapon" I've ever seen.

It was labelled Newfoundland Duck Boat. It was a scrawny rowboat about four metres long featuring what looked like a small cannon mounted on the bow. Apparently nineteenth-century outport Newfoundlanders would stealthily row the boat into a bay filled with hundreds—even thousands—of migrating ducks. Then the oarsman would jump up and wave madly to startle the ducks into flight while his fellow huntsman touched off the buckshot-laden cannon.

If things worked out well, the entire community had duck for the rest of the year.

There were other treasures in that magical cave. I got to try on the breastpiece of a sixteenth-century Scottish suit of armour. I also modelled an ancient Persian helmet like the one Brad Pitt wore in Troy.

Actually I tried to put it on, but the breastplate looked like a brooch and the helmet sat on my head like an acorn. Those guys were really tiny compared to us.

The wonder of it was, all this glorious stuff was just stashed like junk in the ROM attic—barely labelled or sorted. It was the an tithesis of typical museum protocol, where everything is, as D.H. Lawrence lamented, coordinated and systematized.

It was chaos for a museum, but heaven on earth for a teen-aged boy like me.

And now, half a century later, the truth can be told. I'm the guy who broke the flash pan on that exquisite seventeenth-century muzzle-loading flintlock musket.

It was an accident. I was pretending I was the Comte d'Artagnan. Sorry about that.

On the other hand, I had absolutely nothing to do with hiding that dinosaur.